Yosemite
May 8th 1997
Three day trip

WILDFLOWERS

OF

YOSEMITE

By
LYNN & JIM WILSON
AND JEFF NICHOLAS

D0029622

SIERRA PRESS, INC.

P.O. BOX 430, EL PORTAL, CA 95318

Formerly Published by Sunrise Productions

SPECIAL THANKS!

The values presented in this book were instilled in us at an early age. To Barbara and Jim Wilson, Lyn Griffith, Norman and Zoda Moulton, and Jan and Roger Nicholas, our parents and grandparents, we dedicate this wildflower book as a living tribute.

Many wonderful and caring people helped shape and mold this book from its inception. Dr. Carl Sharsmith recognized the seed of interest Lynn and Jim had in botany and took the time to nurture that interest to its first blossom. His guidance and encouragement have been invaluable. Len McKenzie, Yosemite's Chief Park Interpreter, has been a good friend, as well as supportive with ideas and encouragement. Stephen Botti, Vicki Jo Lawson and Paul Gallez spent many hours reviewing our text for content and accuracy. An extra special word of appreciation to Ann Mendershausen for the countless hours fine-tuning the descriptions and eliminating all the "silly" mistakes that amateur botanists are prone to make. Mary Vocelka, Yosemite research librarian, and Norma Craig, of the Park Visuals Center, were of incalculable assistance.

John Poimiroo provided information pertaining to the positive role the Yosemite Park and Curry Company plays in maintaining a healthy floral habitat surrounding their heavily used facilities. Garrett DeBell, Yosemite Park and Curry Company environmental specialist, helped us appreciate how Yosemite's major concessionaire is working to preserve the environment.

Using her word processor, a special young lady, Lea Wilson, took valuable time from her active social life to transform her parents disorganized thoughts into coherent text.

Last, but not least, every author needs a good editor. We were fortunate to find Ardeth Huntington. She not only has command of the English language, but has a deep love and knowledge of Yosemite.

A heartfelt thanks to everyone who touched this project; you were all invaluable!

Photo Credits:
Jeff Nicholas   Front cover, Pages 12, 14 & 16, Plates 3, 4, 7, 24, 34, 38, 44, 47, 48, 49, 59, 60, 67, 72, 84, 87, 100, 110, 112, 116, 132, 137, 140, 148, 149, 151, 152, 158, 171, 177, 179, 180, 183, 186, 187, 189, 196, 201, 203, 205, 210, 214
Raye Santos   Plate 28
E.A. McKinlay   Plates 27, 29, 43, 156, 216, 217
Roger McGehee   Plates 131, 161
National Park Service   Plates 16, 30, 31, 120, 129, 168, 190, 220
Jim Wilson   Back Cover, Pages 13 & 15, Plates—all the rest

Edited by Ardeth Huntington
Design, Map and Illustrations by Jeff Nicholas
First Printing 1987 © Sunrise Productions (Former ISBN 0-961765-10-0)
Second Printing 1990 © Sierra Press, Inc.
Third Printing 1992 © Sierra Press, Inc.

ISBN 0-939365-02-2   Printed in Hong Kong

TABLE OF CONTENTS

The Authors   **Photo by:** Glenn Crosby

ABOUT THE AUTHORS

Jeff Nicholas has been travelling and photographing intimate landscapes throughout the west for eighteen years. The sensitive style of his images reflect his concern for the envirnoment. To his professional credit are two calendars of his own creation; 1987 Living Waters and 1986 Anasazi. Jeff's work has also been selected for use in many other calendars, magazines and postcards; has several posters; plus being included in several photographic books of the west.

Since childhood, both Lynn and Jim Wilson have spent countless vacations exploring Yosemite and the Sierra Nevada—Lynn through the eyes of her photographer/grandfather Norman Moulton. Grandpa created in her a special love for nature, a love you will share throughout this book. Jim has been backpacking in the Sierra Nevada since his youth, providing a deep and firm foundation to his concern for this fragile environment. His love for the wilderness, coupled with his attitude of conservation, stimulates creativity in his photography. In 1984, Lynn and Jim spent three months hiking and photographing the John Muir Trail (Yosemite Valley to Mt. Whitney, 222 miles). Their first book *Sierra Sunrise Along the John Muir Trail,* was published as a result of that odyssey. These three months provided a great deal of time to "stop and smell the roses". As a result, Lynn's past love-affair with the enchanting wildflowers was rekindled.

Jim and Jeff became acquainted in 1985, while living and working in Yosemite. A mutual admiration for Yosemite and a passion for sharing the intimate landscapes led to their co-producing the Yosemite Engagement Calendar. Lynn's love of wildflowers, combined with Jim and Jeff's photographic creativity, inspired this book.

Our wish is that you enjoy Lynn's words together with Jim and Jeff's photographs, gain knowledge of the wildflowers, and in the process become more intimate with the natural environment. Conservation is not just for "someone else". Without a healthy Earth, our culture will soon fail.

Thanksgiving Day, 1986

INTRODUCTION
HOW TO USE THIS BOOK

This book was created as a "user friendly" guide to Yosemite's lovely wildflowers, and as such does not presume a formal education in botany. It is designed to be a simple guide to indentification of Yosemite's most common species of wildflowers. Each plant is discussed in conversational English, presented in photographic form, and its habitat located by specific geographic region. We hope that it will acquaint you further with Yosemite's flowering gems and serve as a primer to your education in botany. This book is intended to be a first step in your gaining a well-rounded knowledge of the Yosemite environment. For additional information on wildflowers we refer you to the bibliography for a list of comprehensive botanical texts. Keep in mind that wildflowers are only a small piece of the whole enviornmental puzzle. Trees, wildlife, insects and mankind are all interdependent for their survival, so in the process of identifying each species of wildflower you encounter, we urge you to keep in mind the delicate balance of nature.

The first section of this book is divided into Yosemite's most visited regions. Each chapter includes a discussion of the more interesting aspects of these areas, and points out some of the best places to find the wildflowers pictured in this book.

The second section has color photographs of selected wildflowers. Since color is usually the first characteristic noticed, the species are presented in their respective color groups: white, yellow, red and blue. These color groups are then subdivided into shapes: simple, daisy, odd, elongated clusters, rounded clusters and vines and shrubs. After you have made a tentative identification from the photograph, refer to section three.

The third section is your aid to simple wildflower verification. It contains a brief description of each pictured species, including the common name, scientific name, and the family to which it belongs. The description, in conversational language, includes leaf shape, size of blossom, height of plant, habitat and blossoming time. A word of caution about common names: a single wildflower may have many different "monikers" applied to it. We emphasize common names as the basis of this book's organization, because most people feel more comfortable with them rather than the scientific Latin names. We have selected the most widely accepted, local, common name for a given plant. However, you may recognize it by another name, for common names vary from locale to locale. When doing further research, always use the scientific Latin name to ensure complete accuracy of identification. Here is an example.

ASTER, YOSEMITE   *Aster occidentalis*   SUNFLOWER FAMILY
                          var. *yosemitanus*

common name   *genus species*   *family name*
                          variety of species (var.) or sub species (ssp.)

If a question arises as to the definition of a phrase or term, refer to the glossary, sketches or a dictionary. We have taken great care to make this book easy to use and hope it makes your wildflower excursions more enjoyable.

1. YOSEMITE OVERVIEW

After even a brief visit to this great Park, it becomes obvious why Yosemite, in 1864, was the birthplace of a revolutionary concept. President Abraham Lincoln was persuaded that our great scenic resources were neither unlimited nor indestructable. He had the courage to do what no man had ever done, to set aside a piece of wilderness, Yosemite Valley and the Mariposa Grove, "for public use, resort and recreation" with the intention that they "shall be inalienable for all time". Over the years his wisdom has proven invaluable, for the United States now has the finest system of National Parks and recreation areas in the world.

The setting aside of Yosemite and the Mariposa Grove proved to be only a first step in the evolution of our modern day concept of conservation and preservation. In 1868, a young Scotsman, John Muir, travelled to the "Range of Light" that had beckoned him from afar. At first, seeking adventure, he hired on as a shepherd in the Yosemite high country. His shepherding tasks took him to the alpine meadows nestled in the mountain range called the Sierra Nevada. Here he had time to study the effect modern man was inflicting on his newly discovered pristine and fragile landscape. These observations eventually led to his intensive endeavors to protect and preserve his beloved wilderness.

John Muir had an unusual affection for these high meadows and their wild inhabitants, which led him into a passionate, acute study of botany. He understood what took the rest of the world another century to comprehend: that all things work together in harmony. He was the first to understand Nature's symphony, realizing that she required all of her "instruments" to orchestrate the complete overture of Life. He studied the snow, how it melted, and where this water went. This snow melt created different watersheds. This led Muir to suggest the idea that what occurred at high elevations would eventually affect the lower valleys. It was obvious to him the mountains surrounding Yosemite were a vital link in the Valley's preservation and needed protection. Through his, and other conservationist's pressure Yosemite's boundaries were expanded and contracted through the years to its present 1,189 square miles.

Yosemite is located in the central portion of the 400-mile-long Sierra Nevada. This mountain range forms the elevated spine that runs almost half the length of California. Due to the unusual heights (up to 14,500-feet), the range acts as an impediment to the flow of winter storms from the west. It is endowed with a unique profile: the western side is a long, gradual slope, while the eastern escarpment is characterized by nearly vertical rises up to 10,000-feet. These factors combine to make the Sierra Nevada an ideal habitat for a diverse representation of plant life.

Altitudes within the Park range from 2,000-feet at El Portal to over 13,000-feet at its eastern crest. Within these wide ranges of elevation are separate communities of plant life, designated by "growth zones". Each zone provides a distinct habitat for the kinds of plants (genera) that occupy a given area. A habitat is distinguished by variables such as temperature, soil condition, moisture and elevation, factors that dictate which genera can exist there.

Some genera have proven to be very adaptable. The **Lupine,** for example, can be found from the sandy coast to higher elevations of the Sierra Crest. Each adaptation produces a separate species of the genus *Lupinus*. The process of adaptation has resulted in 69 different species of **Lupine** in California alone. On the other hand, some genera become a prisoner of their inadaptability. The genus *Oxyria,* for example, can only survive in a very narrow growth zone. Its species, *dignya* **(Mountain Sorrel),** consequently exists as a single member of its genus. **Mountain Sorrel** is not rare however, it is widespread throughout the west, but is restricted to a very narrow habitat.

Our National Parks were set aside as a living laboratory for all to observe and enjoy Nature's ever-changing life cycles. Yosemite, in particular, is a spectacular location. The road and trail system exposes a cross-section of the Sierra Nevada that offers accessability with ease. We, the people, have assigned the responsibility of administrating, studying and protecting our special lands to the National Park Service. It is up to us to enjoy and observe, not collect and destroy. Each time you pick a wildflower you have interrupted Nature's overture, for this instrument of reproduction has ceased its sound of Life. Each time you collect beautiful fall leaves or pine cones, the soil is deprived of their decomposition which provides nutrients for future life. Each time you cut a standing, dead snag you destroy the potential home of the Acorn Woodpecker or Douglas Squirrel. Each time you feed a wild animal you risk signing its death certificate for the following winter. Our own bodies don't deal well with salt, sugar or food additives. Why should we expect wild animals to be unaffected? Even if you went to the hard work of collecting and feeding them their natural foods, you would still have altered nature's overture. You have taught those animals to be dependent on man. This could lead the animals to not store enough for the winter, thus starving them in a season when visitors are not around.

Each National Park has been set aside as a place to observe the interaction and succession of all living things with minimal impact from mankind. The National Park Service has developed guidelines dedicated to this principle, but each visitor must accept the responsibility of adhering to these guidelines. The more you listen, the more you see, the more wonderful the entire overture of Life becomes, and you will find yourself captivated by the symphony Nature is continually playing. Listen, for the quiet is but a movement, and you too become Nature's beautiful instrument, contributing your love and silent respect.

Spring is the time for casting off Winter's chill, and emerging from dormancy. For wildflowers, this rebirth includes a beautiful blossom as a prelude to creating fruit. The spring season begins in Yosemite-area foothills in late February or early March. The hillsides from Briceburg to El Portal along Highway 140 are unsurpassed for early spring displays. The "show" marches gradually up the western slope, culminating, in September, with the intense floral color of the alpine region. Few places in the world offer the casual botanist such a prolonged and diverse wildflower laboratory in which to conduct field studies of Nature's gems. Follow along, in subsequent chapters, as we take a closer look at specific locations where you can find and identify the **WILDFLOWERS OF YOSEMITE.**

Cathedral Spires and Wild Iris, El Capitan Meadow (Chapter 4)

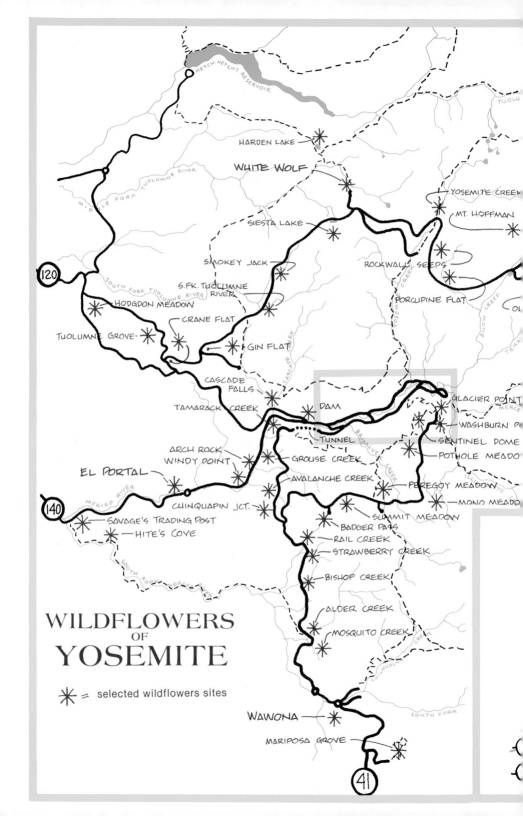

HETCH HETCHY RESERVOIR

HARDEN LAKE

WHITE WOLF

YOSEMITE CREEK

MT. HOFFMAN

SIESTA LAKE

MIDDLE FORK TUOLUMNE RIVER

TUOLU

ROCKWALL SEEPS

SMOKEY JACK

120

SOUTH FORK TUOLUMNE RIVER

S. FK. TUOLUMNE RIVER

PORCUPINE FLAT

SNOW CREEK

OL

HODGDON MEADOW

CRANE FLAT

TENA

TUOLUMNE GROVE

GIN FLAT

CASCADE CREEK

CASCADE FALLS

GLACIER POINT

TAMARACK CREEK

DAM

MERCE

WASHBURN P

TUNNEL

SENTINEL DOME

ARCH ROCK
WINDY POINT

GROUSE CREEK

BADLVER CREEK

POTHOLE MEADO

EL PORTAL

AVALANCHE CREEK

PEREGOY MEADOW

MERCED RIVER

CHINQUAPIN JCT.

MONO MEADO

140

SUMMIT MEADOW

ILLI

SAVAGE'S TRADING POST

BADGER PASS

HITE'S COVE

RAIL CREEK

SOUTH FORK MERCED RIVER

STRAWBERRY CREEK

BISHOP CREEK

ALDER CREEK

WILDFLOWERS
OF
YOSEMITE

MOSQUITO CREEK

CHILNUALNA CREEK

$\ast$ = selected wildflowers sites

WAWONA

SOUTH FORK

MARIPOSA GROVE

41

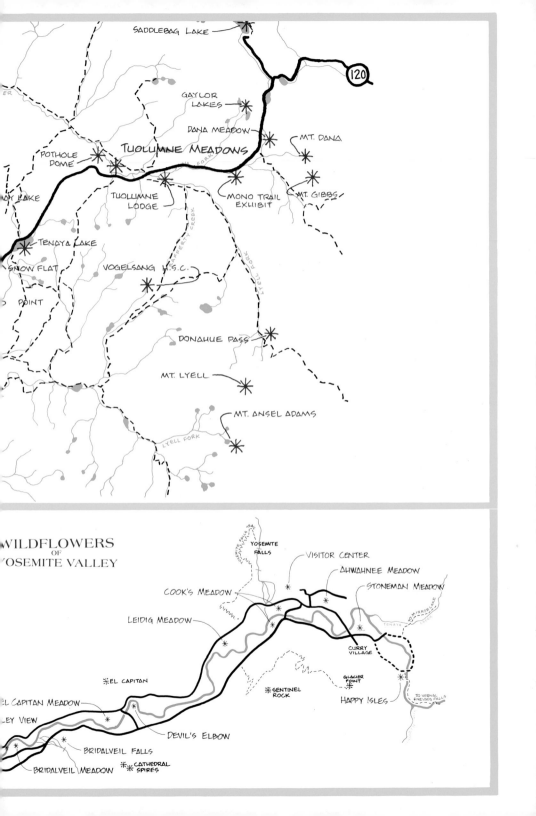

SADDLEBAG LAKE

120

GAYLOR
LAKES

DANA MEADOW

TUOLUMNE MEADOWS

MT. DANA

POTHOLE
DOME

TUOLUMNE
LODGE

MONO TRAIL
EXHIBIT

MT. GIBBS

TENAYA LAKE

SNOW FLAT

VOGELSANG H.S.C.

POINT

DONAHUE PASS

MT. LYELL

MT. ANSEL ADAMS

LYELL FORK

WILDFLOWERS
OF
YOSEMITE VALLEY

YOSEMITE
FALLS

VISITOR CENTER

AHWAHNEE MEADOW

STONEMAN MEADOW

COOK'S MEADOW

LEIDIG MEADOW

TO MIRROR LAKE

TENAYA

CURRY
VILLAGE

EL CAPITAN

GLACIER
POINT

SENTINEL
ROCK

HAPPY ISLES

TO VERNAL
& NEVADA FALLS

EL CAPITAN MEADOW

LEY VIEW

DEVIL'S ELBOW

BRIDALVEIL FALLS

BRIDALVEIL MEADOW

CATHEDRAL
SPIRES

Sierra Rein Orchids, Bigelow's Sneezeweed and Lupine, Crane Flat (Chapter 5)

Wildflower Succession, Lembert Dome and Tuolumne Meadows (Chapter 6)

Shooting Stars, Bistorts, Monkey Flowers, and Corn Lilies, Summit Meadow (Chapter 7)

Mountain Pride Penstemon, Subalpine Habitat, Rafferty Creek

Mountain and White Heather, Vogelsang High Sierra Camp (Chapter 8)

Lupine, Poppies and Goldfields, Merced River Canyon (Chapter 2)

2. YOSEMITE VALLEY TO HITE'S COVE

Highway 120 Jct. to Hite's Cove Trailhead
13.9 miles one way
Hite's Cove Trail 5 miles one way
full day
Peak Season: February to April

In this chapter, our route takes you beyond the traditional boundaries of Yosemite National Park, just west (about 8 miles) of El Portal. The wildflower display of the foothills in spring is considered to be unsurpassed from February to April, well worth the short drive out of the Park.

Our route begins at the Highway 120 intersection (where the dam is located). Don't turn right on Highway 120, toward Tioga Road, instead travel downhill .6 mile until you come to a small level valley at the base of two of the Park's lesser-known waterfalls, Cascade and Wildcat Falls. It is an ideal picnic spot and a favorite place of ours to stop and photograph Wildcat Falls, the smaller and more obscure of the two waterfalls. We particularly like this waterfall in late summer, when the water is low and can be creative photographically, especially with time exposures, for the water slowly splashes over a cascade of shapely rocks. To find Wildcat Falls, walk west about 200 yards from Cascade Falls. This larger waterfall is especially beautiful in early spring, when it is particularly full. Across the road is another large parking area with picnic tables where you can sit and enjoy this captivating scene. You will find **Spice Bush, Mock Orange, Lupine** and **Common Sunflower** growing in this area.

Driving 3.1 miles further down this winding canyon you come to the Arch Rock Entrance Station (named for the overhanging rock formation the road passes through as you enter the Park). You'll find a shady rest area along the river bank, with restrooms and picnic tables.

Past the Entrance Station, the road winds down canyon, following the Merced River. One large turnout at Windy Point (a local name because of the winds of this bend), midway down, offers a spectacular view of the river's many cascades. At the bottom of the hill is "Park Line", a collection of motels and a restaurant. About one mile further you arrive at El Portal. Once a mining town, El Portal is now technically within the Park's boundary. Here is a Park Administration building, grocery store, gas station and the offices of The Yosemite Association. The Yosemite Association is a non-profit organization that assists the National Park Service financially, publishes natural history books, and conducts field seminars in Yosemite. It is located in the Bagby Railroad Station and welcomes visitors.

The El Portal area boasts many species of foothill flowers and in early spring the hillsides are ablaze with the color of **Poppies, Owls Clover, Goldfields, Baby-Blue Eyes, Sierra Nevada Peas,** and **Lupines.** Bordering the Merced River with white and vibrant red are the beautiful **Mock Orange** and **Redbud** shrubs. This spectacular display will take your breath away, but wait, travel another 8 miles to Savage's Trading Post. Named after James Savage who built the original trading post in 1849, this was a place where Indians and miners alike came to trade. It also marks the confluence of the Merced River and its South Fork. Park in the riverside area next to the bridge and across from the modern Trading Post. Take your picnic lunch, water, and lots of film, put on your hiking shoes, and after registering at Savage's Trading Post, prepare yourself for a visual feast.

Follow the Hite's Cove Trail sign, east of the trading post and Redbud Lodge. The trail takes you up a steep dirt incline for a very short way, then becomes level. After only ¼ mile you enter into one of the most diverse and spectacular wildflower displays in the Sierra Nevada. If you have a full day to spend here, don't fail to follow the trail as it winds above the South Fork of the Merced River to Hite's Cove (5 miles), where you will discover the remnants of a gold-mining town. The wealth of minerals uncovered here may have been disappointing, but nature provides a different sort of floral treasure each spring. Every flowering season is different, depending on the weather, but the display usually starts in February and lasts until April, changing with the different habitats along the trail and flowering times for each species.

You'll find from 50 to 60 different species of flowers along this trail but we will describe only a few of them. Because of the uniqueness and floral diversity of this area, a book was devoted to this trail alone, **"Wildflowers of the Hite's Cove Trail"**, by Stephen Botti and Ann Mendershausen. It is available at Savage's Trading Post and was published by the Merced Canyon Committee. The Merced Canyon Committee is devoted to preserving this unique habitat, one of the few undistrubed such environments remaining in which one can observe the results of centuries of plant development.

Most of the trail passes through dry, oak grasslands typical of foothill canyons. In these areas you will find **Poppies, Brodiaeas, Goldfields** and **Chinese Pagodas** (Lynn's favorite). In the shade of spreading Oaks you will find a few flowers that will not wander far from their "umbrella". Nestled beneath are **Indian Pinks, Baby-Blue Eyes** and **Globe Lilies.** Rounding each bend in the trail brings a new and varied fairyland of color.

The moist seep areas along this trail offer a different kind of floral display. Water seeps play hosts to a multitude of species; take time to find them. Lynn likes to sit down

18

on the trail and count the number of different flowers she can find. You, too, can rest in the cool shade and be pleasantly surpurised by the number of species you are able to identify. See if you can find **Monkey Flowers, Shooting Stars, Fiesta Flowers** and **Waterfall Buttercups.** A continuous water supply is necessary for these flowers, so they will not venture far from the seeps and creeks.

Linger here, for as you appreciate each flower and learn its name, you will begin to understand the delicate and special environment you have entered. In time, you become intimately aware of the partnership between one species and another, for in life as in death, Nature has a purpose. We hope to encourage this love for Nature's beauties and stimulate your awareness of the fragility of this environment. While it would seem no harm could come from your picking only one flower or stepping on a single plant, the impact is a *forever* interruption of Nature's progression and plan.

Field Notes

3. YOSEMITE VALLEY TO MARIPOSA GROVE

28.1 miles one way
half day
Peak Season: April to August

The wildflower habitats along this road are numerous and varied. The season lasts longer and supports a more diverse selection than any other region in the Park. Elevations range from 4000-feet in Yosemite Valley and Wawona, to 6800-feet at Wawona Point. Most of the road enjoys a southwest exposure, so receives early spring warmth and sunshine. The dry, well-drained slopes along these stretches encourage growth of many types of shrubs such as **Manzanita, Mountain Misery** and **Chinquapin.** Along Highway 41 (Wawona Road) are creek recesses that alter the wildflower bouquets by the addition of a steady water supply. At the southern terminus of this trip you will find the Mariposa Grove of Giant Sequoias. This Grove of lofty denizens are so spectacular that it becomes difficult to look downward for an equally impressive display of wildflowers. A wildflower excursion along the Wawona Road, coupled with a return trip, should allow plenty of time to stop and explore many different dry areas and numerous creek recesses.

Due to the lengthy blooming season, you may never get to enjoy every wildflower in this region, but there will always be enough available to make the drive pleasurable.

This excursion begins at the junction of Southside Drive and Highway 41 near the Bridalveil Fall parking lot. Driving 1.5 miles up the hill brings you to another large parking area, located at the north end of the mile-long Wawona Tunnel. Ansel Adams immortalized this Tunnel View with his photograph, "Clearing Winter Storm." You may not "see" it the same way Ansel Adams did, but the view is always stunning, regardless of the weather.

Travel 1.7 miles and stop at the turnout next to the rockwall. To the left is Turtleback Dome. A short scamper up the hill reveals a unique view back to Yosemite Valley. From up here notice that Half Dome is now "kissing" El Capitan and seems to loom much larger than at Tunnel View. Alongside the road at the base of Turtleback Dome is an ideal home for **Mountain Pride Penstemon, California Fuchsia** and **Indian Paintbrush.**

As you travel further to the first creek recess, notice that you are passing through a fine stand of **Manzanita.** Later in the season **Sierra Lessingias** color the roadside lavender.

2.4 miles from Turtleback Dome is one of the few places to find the **Washington Lily.** July is the best time to see it in bloom along the road cuts shaded by cedars and pines. It is a favorite browse of deer, so be alert.

After another .2 mile you come to the first of the wet habitats, Grouse Creek. Be sure and explore as many of these creeks as possible, for you will discover new species of flowers at each one. Later in the summer this roadside area is the home of Yosemite's own "star," the **Yosemite Aster.**

1.8 miles past Grouse Creek is Avalanche Creek. This recess hosts the **False Solomon's Seal, Trail Plant, Giant Trillium** and **California Bluebell** (sometimes called **Harebell**). Look along the steep slopes on either side of the road for **Parish's Snowberry** and **Baneberry.**

1.8 miles beyond this refreshing creek is Chinquapin Junction, named for the evergreen shrub found growing prolifically in this area. Examine the bi-colored leaves and the burr-like fruit of this shrub, but be careful, for the burrs are sharp enough to penetrate gloves. The west side of the road is dry — perfect for the **Blue Penstemon** or **Silverleaf Lotus.** The east side of the road is moist from several seeps that encourage a quite different community (see beginning of chapter 7). The road to the left takes you to Badger Pass and Glacier Point. Your route 41, the Wawona Road, continues straight ahead another half mile to a road junction which drops down the hillside on your right into Yosemite West, a private housing development outside the Park boundaries.

For the next 1.4 miles, starting with Rail Creek, you'll encounter another series of creek recesses. Throughout this area are many seep springs that feed roadside displays of **Common Monkey Flower, Lupine, Selfheal** and **Narrowleaf Lotus.**

Strawberry Creek is only .5 mile further, a beautiful and peaceful place to enjoy lunch or a refreshing snack. The area is shaded and cool; a lovely rivulet of water dancing over the rocks makes it an excellent place to find **Indian Rhubarb, Small Leopard Lily, Pinedrops,** and of course its namesake, **Wild Strawberry.**

4.4 miles from Strawberry Creek is a wonderful unnamed seep. Just before and across the road is a turnout with a trash can (Lynn calls it Trash Can Seep). Here you can find a completely different mix of wildflowers from those you've seen at the creeksides. Competing with the tall grasses are the **Tincture Plant, Clarkia, Farewell-to-Spring** and **Common Monkey Flower.** The dryer slopes surrounding this seep display **Lupine** an **Blue Penstemon.**

Mosquito Creek is the last significant creek habitat, 1.2 miles further, and located in the middle of a sweeping hairpin turn. This creek has some different varieties than previously encountered, such as **Wild Ginger, Smoothstem Fireweed, Western Verbena** and **Selfheal,** in addition to many of the previously mentioned species. If time only permits your exploring one creek area, make it this one!

Leave the moist creek recesses behind and drive 4.3 miles to the Wawona area. In addition to varied wildflower habitats, you'll find a pleasantly situated campground, grocery store, gift shop, gas station, the Pioneer History Center and the picturesque old Wawona Hotel. This is a perfect place to pause for refreshment and step back into Yosemite's past. During summer months, you'll find the Pioneer History Center populated with persons enacting roles of pioneers, blacksmiths, soldiers, etc., all eager to converse with you about daily life as it might have been lived during the period from 1890 to 1915, truly a piece of "living history."

Wawona's wildflower display is as varied as its activities. Early in the season, during April and May, the sandy flats become a carpet of blue and white **Miniature Lupines.** June brings the lavender of **Bull Elephants Heads** to the same flats while **Foxgloves, Field Mints** and **Monkey Flowers** bloom alongside the South Fork of the Merced River. The rocky and sandy banks display **Poppies, Mule Ears** and **California Fuchsias. Woolly Mullein** has invaded the meadow and **Mountain Misery** covers the open areas south of the hotel. It doesn't matter whether your interests are flora, romantic accommodations, superb dining, golf, history, or the herd of deer grazing calmly on the meadow — the Wawona area can hold your attention for many hours.

When it's time to leave Wawona, continue 4.7 miles to Yosemite's South Entrance Station. A right turn takes you out of the Park, toward Fresno, but driving straight ahead another 2.1 miles will bring you to one of the great shrines of the Sierra, The Mariposa Grove of Giant Sequoias. The road ends at the parking area in the midst of an impressive grove of the red giants. These trees are neither the oldest nor the tallest trees in the world but no other living thing can claim to be almost 3,000 years old and weigh more than 2 million pounds. Be sure and take the time to explore the Grove. During the vacation season (mid-May to late October) a tram service operated by the Yosemite Park and Curry Company offers tours along the old road, enabling you to see all the great trees at your leisure. If you prefer, hike throughout the forest on a separate trail system. It is easy, in the presence of such denizens, to forget about the diminutive wildflowers growing beneath these giants. In May and June you can find the translucent red **Snow Plant** and, occasionally, **Pinedrops** and **Shinleaf** poking through the rich humus. All three non-chlorophyll-bearing plants are unique in their relationship with the surrounding environment. They were formerly classified as saprophytes, but are now more properly defined as having a mycorrhizal relationship with fungi present in decaying humus (see the description of **Pinedrops**). The thrill of discovering any one of these unique plants will be a memorable experience.

If you find yourself in the Upper Grove late in the afternoon, Wawona Point is a wonderful place to celebrate sunset with a companion. Wawona Point is a short half-mile walk up the spur road from trail marker "S7." Great displays of **Lupine** can be found throughout mid-summer, filling the air with a lovely fragrance. This is one of the few places to combine a view of the Sierra peaks and the Coast Range with a dramatic sunset.

4. YOSEMITE VALLEY

Valley Loop — Beginning At The Visitor Center
14 miles round trip
2 hours
Peak Season: May to August

Your stay in Yosemite National Park will be greatly enhanced by first stopping at the Visitor Center located at the west end of the Village Mall. The National Park Service has done an excellent job of presenting informative displays explaining natural features and the human story of the Park. An information desk is staffed by naturalists who can answer questions and offer suggestions to make your visit more enjoyable.

A short walk across the main road will place you in the middle of one of Yosemite's most prolific wildflower meadows. While strolling to the meadow, don't fail to notice the grove of Black Oak, whose acorns were a main staple of Yosemite's Ahwahnechee Indians. The acorns continue to provide an important food source for most of the Valley's wildlife while the dry, shaded, ground beneath these giants provide an ideal habitat for late-blooming **Sierra Lessingia** and **Gayophytum.**

Step across the road and enjoy the wetland habitat of Cook's Meadow. The show begins in mid-April and extends through September with a steady succession of colorful blossoms. Be prepared for wet feet when observing the early season species since the water table remains high well into summer. April and May bring the creamy-white and yellow of **Western Azaleas**, towering **Cow Parsnips**, a lavender patch of **Shooting Stars** and the beginnings of **Bigelow's Sneezeweed.** As the meadow dries, **Sneezeweed** turns large areas a golden-yellow, soon followed by **Field Mint** and **Indian Pond Lily.** Late May signals the start of a long-running display of the **Showy Milkweed,** ending in October with its seed dispersal in the fall breezes. August begins a crescendo of color with **Narrow Goldenrod, Meadow Goldenrod, Woolly Mullein** and **Bull Thistle** adding their color to those blossoms remaining from earlier in the season.

2.5 miles west on Northside Drive (the one-way road following the north side of the Merced River and leading to all Park exits) you will find Leidig Meadow. This meadow contains waves of tall multi-colored native grasses which blend with species introduced by early settlers to create striking patterns of color and texture. The fringes of this meadow feature an excellent stand of **Indian Hemp.** Its blossoms are small and obscure during summer, but in the fall its leaves create a gold lining to surround the patterned grasses. Yosemite's only species of white violet, **Macloskey's** Violet, can also be found here.

An intimate little picnic area is located .6 mile beyond Leidig Meadow at the apex of a sweeping bend in the Merced River known unofficially as Devil's Elbow. To the east of this picnic area is a small meadow that offers dramatic views of vertical walls and is fill-ed with a delightful variety of colorful flowers. The low area of this meadow supports a small pond throughout spring and in early summer is favored by **Common Monkey Flowers.** On the drying fringes are excellent examples of **Winecup Clarkia, Common Madia, Elegant Brodiaea** and **White Clover.**

Driving .4 mile further brings you to the mecca of rock climbers. El Capitan Meadow is situated between two of the world's most challenging monoliths. Thousands of skilled climbers pilgrimage each year to test their abilities on the vertical walls of El Capitan, Cathedral Rock, and Cathedral Spires. Many Park visitors flock to this meadow to "look up" and stand in awe of the climbers' skill and bravery. For those who admire wildflowers, El Capitan Meadow is a spectacular place to "look down." Throughout the season you will be able to see **Canchalagua, Klamath Weed,** and **Nude Buckwheat** residing on the drying fringe. In the center are long grasses blending with masses of **Narrow Leaf Lotus.** The west end of the meadow features carpets of **Tincture Plants** mingling with **Common Monkey Flowers.** Large mats of white, lacy **Yampah** appear as the meadow begins to dry, while the sunflower-like **Common Madia** blooms on the fr-inge. The flagship of the flowering season in El Capitan Meadow is the **Wild Iris,** also known as **Western Blue Flag,** which sends up distinctive blue, yellow and white blossoms in late April or early May. It is hardy enough to compete with the tall grasses so it can be seen intermingled throughout the meadow. Even in death it can be spec-tacular! In winter, the perpetual shadows of Cathedral Rock transform El Capitan Meadow into a white wonderland. The empty ovaries atop the dried stalks of the Iris pro-vide a cup to catch morning dew. With the freezing temperatures and lack of sun, the dew expands to create crystal rays jetting out from the dried ovary shells. These "Ice Daisies," as Lynn calls them, are one of many in the so-called "Ice Flower Family."

Continuing west 1.6 miles, brings you to a most impressive viewpoint. It used to be known as "Gates of the Valley," for it was the first view of Yosemite Valley visitors saw when arriving via Highway 140 or 120. With the implementation of a one-way road system you only see this view when leaving the Valley, so now it is simply known as "Valley View." In spring and summer this spot is further enhanced by a large variety of wildflowers as well as **Pacific Dogwoods** and **Azaleas** which line the banks of the Merc-ed River.

Walk 200 yards east (back toward the village) and across the road, to see a **Cattail** bog which supports a great number of wetland plants and flowers. Some are as large as the **Creek Dogwood** and some are tiny, such as **Field Mint. Whitestem Hedge Nettle, Ranger Buttons, Cow Parsnips** and **Wild Blackberries** can also be found here throughout the season.

24

Around the next bend, turn left and cross the Pohono Bridge, then proceed a short .8 mile and you will arrive at Fern Spring, the largest of several natural springs in this area. It is the result of a creek far above on the talus slope that disappears into the rocks only to bubble to the surface here prior to joining the Merced River. **Pacific Dogwoods** and **Maples** form a thick canopy over the forest floor, providing cool shade from summer's warm temperatures. Fall brings on the spectacular red and gold leaves these trees are known for, and in the winter the bare trees allow the snowflakes to reach the ground to form a silent and peaceful wonderland. Regardless of when you visit Fern Spring, it will offer the opportunity to feast your eyes on the marvels of time and nature working in unison.

Another .7 mile and you arrive at a place of great historic significance, Bridalveil Meadow, where the Mariposa Battalion camped in 1851. A historic marker commemorates the area where, around a campfire, Yosemite received its modern-day name. 52 years later, in about the same location, seeds of thought were planted for an expanded Yosemite Park and ultimately a National Park system. On that historic evening in 1903 John Muir and Theodore Roosevelt set in motion the conservation movement — one that exists as strongly as ever today. The meadow is no longer an active camping area, but you may walk through it to see the spectacular floral display that occurs each year. Along the creek that divides the grassy flat, you can find **Giant Hyssop, Monkey Flower** and **Field Mint.** The drier portions support **St. John's Wort, Indian Hemp, Lupine** and the lovely **Western Violet.**

1.2 miles from this meadow brings you to the intersection with Highway 41 to Fresno and the parking area of Bridalveil Fall. The Cedar forest adjacent to the parking lot has one of the finest examples of **Western Bleedingheart.** It forms great carpets of lacy green leaves and rose-pink heart-shaped blossoms. Leave the parking lot area, turn right and continue east.

Travel another .9 mile and you will arrive at an impressive view of El Capitan. Park in the turnout and wander through waist high **Lupines, Giant Hyssop** and **Wild Blackberries.** A short distance further you'll come to the Merced River bank where you can find the **Wood Rose,** a distant cousin to our cultivated domestic **Rose.** From here, the distinct view of El Capitan's nose will capture your full attention. This unique view of El Capitan makes a wonderful picture, regardless of whether its in your camera or your memory. But don't let the distraction take your attention from the delicate **Wild Ginger** at your feet. Both the white-veined leaves and the triangular blossoms are well worth the time spent looking for them.

Notice that while driving to the next location, you are passing through a lush Pine forest. In 4.1 miles you will reach the southern portion of Cook's Meadow, an area typical of many such habitats throughout Yosemite Valley. The openings of these forests provide ideal locations for **Deer Brush, Blue Elderberry** and **Mountain Violets.** The thick humus of the conifers provides the perfect place to find non-chlorophyll producing gems such as **Snow Plants, Pinedrops** and **Candy Sticks.**

The fringe area across the road from the Chapel (commonly known as Chapel Meadow) provides ideal growing conditions for several of Yosemite's pretty "weeds." **Coyote Tobacco, Spearmint, Blue Curls, Tower Mustard, Turkey Mullein** and **Hooker's Evening Primrose** grow quite well in the disturbed soil of the roadside.

Each meadow in Yosemite Valley has a wide variety of wildflower species that provide a beautiful floral display each year, but if you can enjoy only one, Stoneman Meadow would have to be the choice! This meadow lies 1.2 miles past the Chapel, between Curry Village and Lower Pines campground. The flowering season begins early, with **Western Azaleas** enhancing the now full Merced River with a stunning floral display. May brings **Cow Parsnip, Yarrow** and the **Common Monkey Flower.** The warmth of summer spurs **Lupine, Milkweed, Black-Eyed Susan, Field Mint** and **Daisy Fleabane.** The later season, August and September, has **Meadow Goldenrod, Sierra Lessingia, Bull Thistle** and **Hooker's Evening Primrose. White Clover** is liberally sprinkled among the grasses and blooms throughout the season. In winter, this meadow blossoms forth with another in the "Ice Flower Family," this species Lynn calls "Cow Lace." The skeletons of Cow Parsnips past are transformed into a unique ice flower. On the end of a stalk is a branched network of smaller stems forming a bowl-shape. Each of these stems also have a branched mini bowl-shaped grouping of stems. This final tiny, umbel skeleton becomes a catch for downy tufts of snow, while the supporting bowl-shaped stems form ice crystals on surviving spider webs weaving an intricate lace pattern.

Last, but not least, on your Valley meadow excursion is the Ahwahnee Meadow, 1.1 miles. Cross Stoneman bridge and follow the road to the first intersection, turn right, pass the Village store, turn right again and park near the Church Bowl. Ahwahnee Meadow has excellent examples of **Common Sunflower, Coyote Mint, Rosy Buckwheat, Moth Mullein, Bull Thistle** and an occasional **Peregrine Thistle.** There is a prolific grouping of **Black-Eyed Susans** in the northeast corner that turns this large area yellow when in full bloom.

A little further down the road is the lavish Ahwahnee Hotel. The interior is tastefully decorated with Indian artifacts and original Indian designs. A tour through this hotel is an excursion through history. The shops offer quality Indian pottery and gifts. The dining is memorable! Informal attire is appropriate for breakfast, brunch, and lunch, but dinner is a special occasion. Don your best evening apparel, or put on your coat and tie or turtleneck and prepare for an evening never to be forgotten, with candle light, live music and superb cuisine. Great care is taken to maintain a high standard for both the guest and the environment. The Yosemite Park and Curry Company, in cooperation with the Park Service, has done an excellent job of careful, elaborate planting of native flowers, making the gardens of the Ahwahnee Hotel a floral extravaganza. The flora around Housekeeping Camp and Curry Village are also a result of this meticulous care, done in accordance with the National Park Service's Natural Resource Management Plan. In no other National Park will you be able to find such fine examples of art, architecture and creative use of native wildflowers.

There remains one final area in Yosemite Valley for you to explore, but you must do it by foot or shuttle bus because private vehicles are no longer allowed to travel these roads. The Happy Isles-Mirror Lake loop is a pleasant half-day hike, bordering a joyous section of the Merced River, as it descends rapidly from Vernal and Nevada falls, leaping and gliding over the huge boulders deposited in the canyon over thousands of years. Like the Fern Spring area, Happy Isles displays the beauty of **Pacific Dogwoods** and **Maples** in addition to providing peace and solitude.

Mirror Lake presents the opportunity to observe "the principle of succession." In the late nineteenth century, early settlers built a small rock dam across a narrow portion of Tenaya Creek, just before it tumbled into the valley. This dam perpetuated Mirror Lake, named because of its perfect reflection of Mt. Watkins. As research scientists learned more about natural processes, it became apparent that the dam was an obstacle to this progression. Consequently, in the early 1970's the dam was removed, allowing the lake to disappear, thus "Mirror Meadow" was born. What you see today is a moist meadow, still in its youth, displaying lovely wildflowers where water once stood. The forested areas along this meadow fringe are full of **Wild Ginger** and the feeder creeks abound with **Waterfall Buttercups.**

Take a moment to reflect on a small lake that once was, the huge granitic formations towering above, and the evolution of a meadow. In spite of mankind's obstructions, Nature will ultimately accomplish her goals of succession. The National Park Service has acknowledged a need to be sensitive to the natural processes, while still providing for the enjoyment of Yosemite's visitors. It is a delicate balance that must be met, and most of Yosemite's three million guests each year agree that our administrators have done an admirable job.

Field Notes

5. YOSEMITE VALLEY TO GIN FLAT

13.4 miles one way
half day
Peak Season: June to August

Chapter 5 offers a compact excursion designed to introduce several impressive wildflower habitats without requiring a lot of driving or physical exertion. Your route starts at the junction of Highways 120 and 140, seven miles west of Yosemite Village. The elevation ranges from approximately 3900-feet (the junction) to 6700-feet (Gin Flat). Most of the habitats discussed are meadow and meadow fringe communities that developed due to a steady supply of moisture.

There is a parking area at the intersection of Highway 120 and 140, two of Yosemite's major entrance roads, across from the small diversion dam. This can be a delightful place for a rest stop in spring or summer and becomes the place where visitors seek "fall gold" in October. The **Maples,** Cottonwoods and **Dogwoods** put on a spectacular show of color during the fall season but springtime should not be overlooked. In addition to the tender green of new leaves, the **Maples** produce "tassels," and the **Dogwoods** creamy blossoms. Turn right and drive up the hill on Highway 120.

Immediately prior to the first tunnel, 1.7 miles from the junction, you can take advantage of a small turnout where you will find good examples of the **Manzinita** in the dry, rocky and exposed environment it prefers. Here also lives a curious and obscure member of the SUNFLOWER FAMILY, **Stephanomeria.** It is a blue to lavendar flower, on long, multi-branched stems, that blooms in July and August. In Yosemite it grows only around this location; and, since its common name is the same as its scientific genus and somewhat difficult to remember, Lynn dubbed it **"Tunnel Flower."**

A series of seep spring habitats begin 3.0 miles beyond the **Tunnel Flower.** These small springs produce an oasis around which many species congregate. Some fine examples of the **Crimson Monkey Flower, Red Clover** and **Tomcat Clover** can be observed.

Another 4.8 miles brings you to Crane Flat, a lush, mid-elevation meadow where Highway 120 divides. During the peak visitation season (May to October) a grocery store and gas station are open at this intersection and .2 mile north, you will find the large Crane Flat campground, making this a delightful camping experience away from the crowds of Yosemite Valley.

The geologic origin of both Crane Flat and Gin Flat are not yet fully understood. It is obvious, though, that they were not formed through glaciation since both occupy ridge-top locations. More study is needed before their beginnings can be more fully comprehended. The lower end of Crane Flat, near the store, supports a thriving community of wetland wildflowers. Here you can find **Sierra Rein Orchids, Bistorts, Checker-mallows, Wild Geraniums, Common Monkey Flowers, Giant Hyssops** and **Shooting Stars.** Towering above its peers is the "king" of Crane Flat, the **California Coneflower.** It stands on stout stems swaying in the gentle breezes and wearing a golden crown. As the moist areas become dry and the golden glow fades, **Yampah** blooms and turns the flats into a creamy-white lacework.

Our route turns right toward Tioga Pass and proceeds 1-mile beyond the grocery store to the upper end of Crane Flat. Because the grassland slopes gently upward from the store, this end of the meadow dries much sooner. While the lower portion is still moist and vibrant, this margin area is blooming with quite different species. **Broadleaf Lupines, Velvety Stickseeds (Sierra Forget-Me-Nots), Angelicas, Ranger Buttons** and **Orange Agoseris** blend their colors into a fringe bouquet. Green is an unusual color for a wildflower blossom but Crane Flat is the home for two such species. **Deers-Tongue** (also known as **Monument Plant**) can be found growing up to 5-feet tall. You can find the four-petaled green blossoms located at the axils. The other green flower is the **Corn Lily,** so named because the spiked flower clusters at the end of the hardy stalks reminded settlers of a cultivated corn field in tassel. The "corn fields" at Crane Flat are truly impressive sights!

An optional side trip that passes through the Tuolumne Grove of Giant Sequoias departs Highway 120 East, .3 mile from here. This Grove has a smaller, but no less impressive, display of Big Trees than the Mariposa Grove. Located in the Tuolumne Grove is the only remaining tunnel tree in Yosemite. The forest floor in a Redwood Grove provides an ideal environment for **Snow Plants, Shinleaf** and **Lupines.** The one-way road continues beyond the Grove through a lush forest of Cedars, Pines and **Dogwoods** to rejoin Highway 120 at the Hodgden Meadow-Big Oak Flat Entrance Station. It is a 13 mile round trip and, time permitting, should not be bypassed.

Three miles beyond the upper end of Crane Flat is Gin Flat. The name has persisted through generations from a single dubious incident. It is said that an early freight wagon inadvertently dropped a barrel of gin while passing through. Sometime later a gathering of cowboys, shepherds and roadworkers threw a "gin party" that is still remembered today! The gin is gone but in its place is a spectacular garden.

The upper portion of Gin Flat is drier and produces great carpets of color. Early June brings the purple mass of **Bridge's Gilia,** in July an ocean of **Yampah** takes over, and August adds the yellow of **Meadow Goldenrod.** Throughout most of the season **Dusky Horkelia** can be found mingling with **Lupines** on the fringe. Across the road, on the low side, is a wet habitat. Here you can find **Primrose Monkey Flowers, Bigelow's Sneezeweed, Sierra Rein Orchids** and **Hooded Ladies Tresses.**

Gin Flat has been chosen as an arbitrary end to this section, but if time permits, it should not signal the end of your journey. Highway 120 East continues to Tuolumne Meadows and is detailed in Chapter 6.

6. GIN FLAT TO TUOLUMNE MEADOWS

36 miles one way
Harden Lake trail 5.6 miles round trip
all day
Peak Season: July to mid-September

The variety and habitat of this description parallels that of chapter 7 since the elevation and direction of the Tioga Road is the same as the Glacier Point Road, with only the spectacular 3000-foot deep gorge of Yosemite Valley separating them.

The previous chapter left you at Gin Flat; this one continues from that location, travelling from west to east along the Tioga Road. It is the only trans-Sierra highway between Bakersfield and Manteca and the only eastern entrance to Yosemite National Park. The Tioga Road opens around Memorial Day (weather permitting) and remains open until the first major storm after mid-October. The elevation varies from 6700-feet at Gin Flat to 8600-feet in Tuolumne Meadows. Your route begins in thick Pine Forests, passes through magnificent Red Fir forests, and finishes in subalpine Lodgepole Pine forests. This corridor has a wide variety of shrubs and wildflowers creating a season-long display of color.

3.3 miles east of Gin Flat is a small "pocket meadow" on the right-hand side of the road. This meadow is tiny, but can be counted on for an impressive show of **Shooting Stars** soon after the snow melts. As the purple carpet fades, **Bigelow's Sneezeweed** takes its place. Since many of the large meadows throughout the Sierra are accessible by road, it is easy for automobile passengers to overlook the tiny pocket meadows. They are a familiar sight to backpackers though, and most hikers have learned to watch for the intimate, floral displays they produce.

Another half mile brings you to a refreshing stop as well as a significant wildflower habitat. Stop at the large turnout on the right, just across the bridge on the South Fork of the Tuolumne River. Walk under the bridge to the water's edge to see **Creek Dogwood** and **Spiraea.** We want to add a word of caution, for the water polished rocks are smooth and slippery, and even when the water level is low, can present a danger. Near the bridge, on the cut roadbanks, are fine examples of **Spreading Dogbane** and **Bloomer Goldenbrush.** The hillside one mile further east, has a sparse representation of **Washington Lily,** a certain surprise in this dry forest environment.

1.8 miles from the South Fork bridge is the site of the old Smoky Jack campground (road marker T-6) which is now closed and being allowed to return to its natural state. Across from this former entrance road is a colorful display of **Monkey Flowers, Wandering Daisies, Pearly Everlasting, Shooting Stars, Bistorts** and **Asters.**

Travelling 3.4 miles from Smoky Jack brings you to moist areas on both sides of the road between a stately stand of Red Fir. The nearby roadcuts provide an ideal dry environment for **Shieldleaf** and the brilliant red of **Scarlet Gilias.** The creekbank nearby is typical of many creeks at this elevation. **Bistorts, Shooting Stars,** the less common **Small Leopard Lilies** and **Green Rein Orchids,** mingle with the grasses, while **Mountain Lungwort** and **Arrowleaf Senecio** tower above.

.8 mile further is Siesta Lake, a shallow basin that catches snow melt and forms a sleepy little pool. The shoreline has excellent examples of **Brewer's Lupine, Asters** and **Sulphur Flowers.** Around every bend intense purple color captures your attention, from the tiny carpet of **Brewer's Lupine** to the large, bush-like, **Broadleaf Lupine.**

Another mile further, just prior to the White Wolf junction, is a rocky roadside that supports **Spiraea, Wandering Daisies, Asters, Mountain Pennyroyal** and **Pearly Everlasting.** Roadside cuts such as this one present a curious blend of plants. The environment seems to be dry and gravelly, but the runoff from summer thundershowers provide ample moisture to sustain some wetland species as well. Even with manmade disturbances of soil, nature takes the opportunity to show off.

At the White Wolf junction, depart the Tioga Road briefly and drive one mile to this High Sierra Camp. Here you'll discover, in addition to the campground, a lodge, a simple high-country restaurant, a small store and lush meadows. The moist grass area contains carpets of **Meadow Penstemon** and **Bull Elephants Head,** while the drying fringes display the diminutive **Tinkers Penny** and **Locoweed.** If time permits, hike the trail down to Harden Lake (5.6 miles round trip). The trail follows a year-round creek with stands of **Arrowleaf Grounsel, Spiraea, Small Leopard Lily** and **Shieldleaf.** Around Harden Lake, **Coralroot** and **Snowplant** poke through the humus-rich forest floor. Continue along the right side of this lake, down a set of switchbacks, and behold Harden Gardens, usually at its peak flowering season in early August. This pocket meadow has unusually large numbers of species and, for the amateur botanist, is a real treat to visit.

3.5 miles beyond the White Wolf junction is a series of turnouts which allow observation of **Scarlet Penstemon, Mountain Pride, Indian Paintbrush** and the late-blooming **Wright's Buckwheat.** These species prefer the well-drained, sandy soil that this stretch of southerly exposed road provides.

Proceed 1.8 miles further to Yosemite Creek. The water passing under this bridge will soon be crashing over the brink of the north Valley wall, forming 2425-foot Yosemite Falls. Here the sandy roadbanks support a bright red bouquet of **Scarlet Penstemon.**

The next 3 mile section of Tioga Road presents one of the most incredible roadside displays in the Park! At the Quaking Aspen exhibit you'll find **Thimbleberry, Fireweed, Creek Dogwood** and **Spiraea**. Continuing from this point is a "rock wall seep" (on the map), which Lynn calls "Tioga's Hanging Gardens." Water draining from the hillside above combines with the exposed soil from road construction to create a community of strange bedfellows. Where else in Yosemite can you find **Pink Monkey Flowers, Lupines, Pearly Everlasting, Indian Paintbrush** and **Blue Penstemons** growing side by side? If that isn't enough, the parking area across the road from these gardens have the white tufts of **Nude Buckwheat,** yellow **Sulphur Flowers** and pink **Pussypaws,** making "Tioga's Hanging Gardens" an adventure in botany all by itself.

4.3 miles beyond the end of "Tioga's Hanging Gardens" a side road veers to the left. Across from this road, on the right, is a drive-through turnout. Located below this tur- nout, nestled in the sweeping right bend of the Tioga Road, is an unofficially named lake, known to most as "Weston Lake," after the photographer Edward Weston. Both Edward and his son Brett have created stunning images of this lake. For photographers, this lake presents creative challenges with its (seemingly) "floating rocks." For wildflower enthusiasts, it provides a handsome, profuse, display of **Labrador Tea** en- compassing its shores.

After exploring "Weston Lake," cross the Tioga Road and drive 1.8 miles to the May Lake trailhead. Along this road you will see **Coulter's Daisy, Meadow Rue, Marsh Marigold, Wandering Daisy** and **Corn Lily.** The 1.2-mile-long foot-trail to May Lake rewards you with an azure-blue high-country lake. Here also is another of the High Sierra Camps operated during the summer by the Yosemite Park and Curry Company. The camps are located on the High Sierra Loop Trail and offer, by advance reservation, meals and lodging to backcountry hikers. The small store has some refreshments and you may purchase a welcome shower. May Lake marks the beginning of the trail to the summit of Mt. Hoffman, the geographical center of the Park. Its summit is another 2 miles further and offers the ambitious hiker some rewarding views as well as a brief in- troduction to alpine botany (chapter 8). This rocky habitat is a perfect playground for the cute marmots residing there.

Returning to the Tioga Road, travel 2.3 miles further to Olmsted Point, for an over- whelming view south to Half Dome and Clouds Rest. An ironic twist: after travelling more than fifty miles you are finally in a position to see the same granite monoliths you left a few hours ago! While pondering this situation, wander around the magnificent granite above the road for an opportunity to see **Indian Paintbrush, Sulphur Flowers, Mountain Pride, Pussypaws** and Yosemite's own species of **Bitterroot.** Also notice the stately specimens of Western Juniper, a twisted but sturdy tree that is well suited to cold winters and dry summers.

The large lake that lies 1.7 miles ahead is Tenaya Lake, named in honor of the Chief of the Ahwahnechee. When told of this "honor," Chief Tenaya claimed the lake already had a name — Py-we-ack or "the lake of shining rocks." As you travel the edge of the lake, where the granite meets the road, notice the glacial polish and you'll understand why the original inhabitants chose "Py-we-ack."

Another 4.2 miles brings you to the crown jewel of the Sierra, Tuolumne Meadows, the largest meadow in the range. The road follows this meadow for 3 miles, with trails branching off toward impressive vistas which can only be seen by foot travel. At 8600-feet above sea level, this meadow presents an ideal laboratory to study the subalpine flora. The medley of flowers seem almost endless. Early in the season, the moist grassy areas display a lavender carpet of **Alpine Shooting Stars.** As the ground begins to dry, the **Shooting Stars** fade and **Meadow Penstemons** take their place, then **Lemmon's Paintbrush** and **Little Elephants Heads** succeed **Penstemons.**

This process ends with the approaching fall season (see page 13). Mingling among these beautiful flowers is the less conspicuous but equally impressive **Rose Everlasting.** True to its name, it will still be around long after the other flowers have faded. A word of caution: the meadows remain damp throughout the summer season, so please be careful where you place your boots. Another generation of wildflowers are waiting to succeed the one you may now be admiring. At these elevations it takes as long for the meadows to regenerate severe damage as a forest takes to reach maturity.

The shaded ground beneath the Lodgepole Pines provides an ideal habitat for **Mariposa Lilies, Wild Strawberries, Crimson Columbines, Alpine Gold Brodiaea, Pale Agoseris, Heartleaf Arnicas, Sierra Wallflowers, Dwarf Louseworts, Single-Stemmed Groundsels** and **Shieldleaf.** They don't share the same location, but are usually close neighbors. A little searching should reveal most of them and more.

To experience all of Tuolumne Meadows in a few short hours is impossible. We have had a love affair with this area for years; we never stop seeing new places, or experiencing old places in a different way.

For the convenience of a longer stay you'll find a large campground, well-stocked grocery store, gas station, mountaineering shop, and Tuolumne Lodge, another in the series of High Sierra Camps, complete with small gift shop, showers and restaurant. Advance reservations made through Yosemite Park and Curry Company offers you an opportunity to experience this particular wilderness area without hiking to get there.

Tuolumne Meadows tantalizes you with an introduction to the beauty of high country wildflowers, but a tease is all it is. Want to see more? Drive 7 miles further to Tioga Pass. Want to see more than that? Plan a hike to the summit of Mt. Dana, beginning at the Tioga Pass Entrance Station. See chapter 8 for a description of the alpine country, but be forewarned: you must experience it to fully appreciate it. For now, linger in these meadows a while longer, where time stands still, and cares are blown away with the gentle alpine breezes.

7. CHINQUAPIN TO GLACIER POINT

16.5 miles one way
Sentinel Dome trail 1.1 miles one way
Taft Point trail 1.1 miles one way
half day
Peak Season: mid-June to mid-August

The habitat encountered along the Glacier Point Road is similar to that found along Highway 120 to Tuolumne Meadows. The elevation range falls between 6,000-feet (Chinquapin) and 8,122-feet (Sentinel Dome), passing through Red Fir and Lodgepole Pine forests.

At the junction of Chinquapin and the Glacier Point cut off, is a fine example of one of the most intimate and stunning seeps found in the Park. From the rest area at the junction, walk a short distance (300 yards) toward the Valley. Rocks often drip precious pure snow-melt and form dazzling seep-springs. The springs bubble forth, seemingly from nowhere, disappearing as gently as they arrived, leaving behind a lushly colored quilt as their tribute.

The water inspires a soft mattress of **Star Moss** covering the ground at the base of a display of more majestic flowers. Towering above are **Scarlet Monkey Flowers, Narrowleaf Lotus, Sierra Rein Orchids** and **Coneflowers.** Deep-green ferns mingle freely to complete the royal setting.

Now turn onto the road to Glacier Point, knowing that flower treasures are often tiny and easily overlooked. In 2.9 miles, notice another seep on the right side of the road, while the left side supports a drier habitat. Here a different flora is encountered. The **Broadleaf Lupine, Spreading Dogbane, Mountain Lungwort,** and **Parish's Snowberry** huddle beneath giant Red Firs.

From here drive 2.4 miles further to the Badger Pass turn-off. Badger Pass is known as an excellent family ski center in the winter. In summer, the ski trails are transformed into Monroe Meadows, named in honor of a stagecoach driver who worked for the Washburn's stage line. Their stages originally traveled a different route, further east, than today's modern road, and finally ceased operation in 1875 when the new and still existing road was completed into Yosemite Valley.

1.2 miles beyond this intersection is Summit Meadow, Nature's playground of wildflowers. Rarely does this moist meadow completely dry, so the peak of the season seems to last much longer. Early in its flowering time you may find **Bistorts, Shooting Stars, Camas Lilies,** and **Sierra Rein Orchids.** Later, **Cow Parsnips, Bigelow's Sneezeweed** and **Corn Lilies** join the floral bouquet.

Travel another 1.9 miles to Peregoy Meadow- Bridalveil Creek Campground. This meadow, on both sides of the main road, was named after Charles E. Peregoy, who operated "The Mountain House," an early hotel located ¼ mile beyond. He, too, ceased operating the hotel with the completion of the new road. Peregoy Meadow dries early in the summer and has an impressive field of **Larkspur. Yampah** also is quite prevalent, although it appears later in the season.

The Clark Range comes into view in another 2.8 miles. This vista is breathtaking! Look eastward for your first view of Yosemite's eastern alpine region (Chapter 8). Here, sun-drenched slopes and the absence of towering trees encourage the growth of **Manzanita.**

Just 2.4 miles further Pothole Meadows, to your left, plays peek-a-boo through the conifers. These lush meadows contain unique, round pools, about 5-feet in diameter, whose origin is still not completely understood. As the snow melts and while the meadows are still marshy, an expanse of lavender **Shooting Stars** obscure the early green of the meadow grasses. Around the drier fringes grow an abundance of **Corn Lilies** and **Arrowleaf Groundsel.**

Leaving the last of the subalpine meadows behind, the road breaks out into a sudden clearing and you see your first view of Sentinel Dome. A parking area is only another .4-mile. Park your vehicle here and enjoy a 1.1-mile walk to the top of Sentinel Dome or a 1.1-mile walk to Taft Point. As you follow the trail from the parking area, notice the dead tree (parts of it are both standing and on the ground). This stump is a prime example of Nature using death to sustain life, for in the holes are found woodpecker nests and in early summer you can watch the parents fly food to their young.

If you turn left, the trail will take you to Taft Point. This trail goes through a wet bog area in the midst of Red Firs harboring abundant **Corn Lilies, Arrowleaf Groundsel, Sulphur Flower** and **Sierra Wallflower.** Descending out of this forest the trail becomes steep and exposed. Near the base of this hill are the five fissures. This interesting view is dangerous because of all the loose gravel and caution need be taken when nearing the edge. We have viewed different raptors soaring the cliffs and watching our intrusion on their domain with keen interest. Just beyond the fissures is the point. Taft Point juts out giving a 180 degree panorama and an especially impressive view of the gliders landing.

If you chose Sentinel Dome you will veer right at the dead tree. From the bridge crossing the young Sentinel Creek, step gently in either direction for an impressive display of **Kelly's Tiger Lilies,** and **Spiraea.** With diligent searching (and some luck) you may find the diminutive, intricate blossoms of **Davidson's Fritillary,** found in the wooded area surrounding the creek.

This walk becomes more difficult as you get close to its completion, but the rewards soon overcome your fatigue as you find a spectacular 360 degree panorama of Yosemite's high country spread out before your eyes. The peacefulness you experience here is magnified with this vast expanse and the silence is broken only by the wind's whisperings and the distant thunder of Vernal and Nevada Falls seen in the background, plunging over their granite aprons. Even in death, the lonely Jeffrey Pine commands attention with its beauty. At sunset the warm tones of twilight soften its remaining bark to a burnt-orange hue. The rich colors of alpenglow are seen reflecting off Clouds Rest, North Dome, Mount Hoffman and especially Half Dome. The Clark Range turns a stunning pink while Red Peak is seemingly ablaze. Thus begins the night. Stars grace the dark expanse with a brightness and profusion not often seen by most people. So bright it is, in fact, that you can find your way by star-light alone, however Sentinel Dome by moonlight is an experience never to be forgotten!

It may be hard to tear yourself away from Sentinel Dome's views, but another marvelous experience awaits you at Washburn Point, only 1.5 miles beyond. Sunrise here is unsurpassed: silhouettes of peaks on the horizon, the crashing thunder of Vernal and Nevada Falls looming below, and the chill of morn all stimulate anticipation. As the warming orb begins its ascent, prisms of sunlight turn clouds into an eruption of fire. Low on the monolithic granite, creeping pillows of fog rise to meet the sun, forming rings around Half Dome's hidden brow. As the sun warms the new day, the fog lifts to reveal its overwhelming closeness. Mornings like this are uncommon, but never forgotten.

The final ½ mile brings you to Glacier Point. Park here and follow a short, paved trail to the lookout with its stunning views of Half Dome and beyond. Here is the area where hang gliders push off, the first step in a thrilling descent to the Valley floor. This Ranger-supervised activity is scheduled early in the morning (usually on weekends) when a window of calm air currents occur. From the launch point you can watch these colorful, man-made wings circle over Vernal and Nevada Falls; but to watch them soar between Yosemite's vertical cliffs, you must scamper out to the tip of Glacier Point.

With the dramatic views from Glacier Point, this description ends. But it signals the beginning of the same visual sights in reverse order. ENJOY!

8. THE ALPINE

Tuolumne Meadows to Saddlebag Lake
10.7 miles one way
2 hours
Peak Season: July to August

This chapter is titled "The Alpine" but most of the areas described are not truly alpine country. Strictly defined, the alpine region doesn't begin until you've left the last tree behind. The most accessible subalpine and alpine zones in Yosemite are located near Tuolumne Meadows. The following route continues from Chapter 6 beginning at the intersection of Tioga Road and the spur road (right) to the Tuolumne Ranger Station. It is 5.7 miles from this junction to the entrance gate at Tioga Pass. Along the way are many turnouts with fine examples of **Brewer's Lupine, Alpine Goldenrod, Alpine Shooting Star, Dwarf Bilberry** and **Alpine Willow.** Stop at your convenience and enjoy the floral displays as they occur.

At the entrance station take the time to wander along the road on either side of the crest and observe the community that has adapted to this harsh environment. The disturbed soil supports **Alpine Dandelion, Brewer's Lupine, Tioga Thistle, Alpine Monkey Flower, Alpine Goldenrod** and **Mountain Clover.**

Exit the Park and continue down the east side of Tioga Pass 3 miles (just beyond Tioga Pass Resort) to a junction with a dirt road on the left. Follow this dirt road 2 miles to Saddlebag Lake. Like May Lake (Chapter 6), it is a fine example of a high country lake which supports an abundant array of wildflowers. This region has good specimens of **Western Roseroot, Alpine Monkey Flower** and **Grass-of-Parnassus.**

For the curious and ambitious the only remaining zone to explore is the alpine. It is time to lace up the hiking boots and set off for the summit of Mt. Dana, elevation 13,053-feet! The trail is 5.8 miles round trip and quite strenuous, but the rewards are both satisfying and infectious. One trip to the alpine is never enough. Once infected you must return time and time again. There is a mystical attraction to both the challenge and the beauty of this "world above the trees." Wildflowers in this region have been forced to meet this challenge or disappear forever. Most alpine varieties have adapted by developing a low profile to avoid the persistent winds. Some have adapted by becoming perennials. They have developed hardy rootstocks or remain evergreen beneath the heavy snowpack, only to spring forth with fresh blossoms the instant winter snows melt. Their color is more vibrant, apparently to more easily attract the attention of a reduced number of natural pollinators. All these factors combine to create some unique versions of the more familiar genera of lower elevations.

The trail to Mt. Dana begins at the Tioga Pass Entrance Station and immediately strikes for the summit. At the base of Mt. Dana is a pocket meadow of stunning subalpine flowers. Found growing here are tall versions of **Broadleaf Lupine, Tower Larkspur, Swamp Onion, Indian Paintbrush** and **Arrowleaf Groundsel,** a lush display of waist-high finery. From this garden the trail ascends steeply to Lynn's "False Summit Plateau," marked by a rock pylon 3 feet tall. Along the way, **Sierra Arnica, Spreading Phlox** and **Alpine Buckwheat** line the trail. Close scrutiny will also bring some very special species to your attention. The rocky area below the Lying Head (a steep abutment at the north end of "False Summit Plateau") is a prolific area for lovely **Coville's Columbine.** Its creamy-white erect heads stand unusually tall in the winds, hoping to attract pollinators. **Steers Head** is another of the special flowers that can be found here, but it almost requires searching on your hands and knees. Find a melting snowbank with fine gravelly soil beneath it. Each blossom only lasts about a week, but as the flowers of one elevation are fading, they are blooming at the next higher elevation. The alpine blooms appear progressively higher and higher giving you ample opportunity to locate them. It takes diligent searching, but finding **Steers Head** is worth the effort.

"False Summit Plateau" and the alp just below it are excellent locations for finding **Davidson's Penstemon, Cut-Leaved Daisy, Mountain Sorrel** and **Dana's Lupine** (Mt. Dana's own variety). At this point the trail becomes nonexistent and you must choose your own arduous route to the summit. While struggling in the thin air of this last steep climb, keep in mind that two floral gems await your discovery. The first to be encountered will be **Alpine Gold.** This daisy-like, yellow flower stands proudly erect on a 16-inch stem, ready to face any condition that nature can produce.

As **Alpine Gold** declines to advance further uphill, only one species remains to brave the summit: **Sky Pilot** is truly the "king of the mountain." It is a hardy little plant that was named after the mythical person who assisted others to Heaven from the loftiest peaks. The elements dictate the **Sky Pilot's** life cycle to be slow and deliberate. It can take twenty years to send up its first blossom and will live to be a century old if not disturbed. Records indicate that at one time the entire summit area was covered with **Sky Pilot's** blue blossoms, but over the years many people have intruded on its habitat. A misplaced boot or two is all that is required to eliminate one of these jewels from existence, so please be careful! Linger awhile and admire the majestic views from the top — at this point you've earned it.

An alternate journey into the alpine region is the hike to Vogelsang High Sierra Camp. The trip from Tuolumne Meadows up Rafferty Creek to Vogelsang, and down Ireland Creek to the Lyell Fork of the Tuolumne River and back covers 20.5 miles and is a moderate 2- to 3-day backpack trip. If this is your first overnight trip onto the high country you are in for the treat of your life. The moon and stars are spectacular, as are the wildflowers, at Vogelsang. The rock gardens around the camp support **White Heather, Mountain Heather, Sierra Primrose** and **Rockfringe.** The moist meadow area has **Alpine Paintbrush, Little Elephants Head, Alpine Laurel, Alpine Gentian** and **Lemmon's Paintbrush.**

It is difficult to express our love for the alpine, for all of Yosemite is our "favorite place" and all the flowers are our "favorite flowers." Each place, each flower, is the most captivating at that particular moment, and they then become our "favorite." But the alpine — captures the heart and releases the mind to never-dreamed-of splendor: snow-capped granite, harboring pocket meadows with the most intense color imaginable. The brightness and clarity of midnight stars. The morning light, pink against looming mountains. This — is the alpine! Be prepared to be smitten with the "alpine bug," for it takes but a brief stay here to yearn for more.

9. What's In A Name?

There are almost 350,000 species of plants in the world, ranging in size from microscopic algae to gigantic Redwoods. When confronted with such quantities and diversity the human mind attempts to make order out of this chaos. It is not surprising, therefore, that throughout the ages man has tried to classify the plant world, using a variety of criteria including size, habitat, and use.

Our modern system of plant taxonomy (the science of classification) dates back to the 18th Century, when a Swedish doctor/botanist, Carolus Linnaeus, devised a superior system. Linnaeus observed that the reproductive structures of a plant (its flowers, fruit, and seeds) remained more or less the same. They were not affected by external factors as were the plants vegetative structures (its leaves, stems, and roots). From this observation, he created a system of classification based on plant reproductive structures. Today's classification schemes go even further by attempting to reflect the generic relationships of plants (their evolutionary history). Classifying is a continual process, ever-changing in response to increasing botanical information.

Linnaeus also standardized the naming of plants by introducing a binomial system (two names) in which every plant has two Latinized, scientific names. For example, the **Irish Potato** is *Solanum tuberosum. Solanum* is the name of the genus (group of related species) and *tuberosum* describes the species (plants of one kind). People who are accustomed to common names often think Latinized names are too "scientific" for everyday use, and are hard to pronounce and remember. But stop and think for a moment: you don't hesitate to say *"Rhododendron"* or *"Chrysanthemum,"* both of which are Latinized generic names.

We all use common names for plants, but we should realize that they have serious drawbacks. Scientific nomenclature has become standardized globally, whereas common names have not. For example, in England the common name "Corn" refers to Wheat, in Ireland to Oats, and in the United States to Maize. If you want to discuss botany with fellow admirers around the world, common names will be insufficient and it becomes imperative to know some scientific Latin names.

Scientific botanical names also give descriptive information about a plant. In the case of the **Irish Potato,** *Solanum* (which means "quieting") refers to the narcotic properties of some members of the genus and *tuberosum* tells you that the plant has tubers (fleshy, underground stems, the "Potatoes"). Common names, on the other hand, often give misinformation about a plant. **Owls Clover** *(Orthocarpus purpurascens)* is not a clover at all: it is related to Snapdragons, and owls certainly do not feed upon it!

In the hierarchy of the plant kingdom, "species" indicates plants of one kind, "genus" (plural, genera) indicates a group of related species, and "family" includes related genera. Just as members of human families often have distinguishing characteristics, so do plant families. All members of the MINT FAMILY, for example, tend to have two-lipped flowers, opposite leaves, square stems and be aromatic. Plants in the MUSTARD FAMILY are characterized by pungent sap, alternate leaves, four petals and four sepals, and distinctive seedpods. Plant size, however, is not a familial characteristic, for within a single family you may find herbs, shrubs, and trees. Therefore, it is primarily the structure of the flower that indicates the family relationship.

With practice, you will be able to acquire a "feeling" for some plant families, and even for certain genera. Identifying a plant to the species level is often difficult, even for professional botanists, so don't be discouraged if you make a few mistakes. The time and effort it takes to become familiar with plants is doubly repaid by the pleasure and beauty they bring to your life. Begin by learning the plants in your own back yard. Then when you travel — to a National Park or to a foreign country — seeing a familiar plant face will make you feel less of a stranger. It is a wonderfully satisfying experience to be in a foreign land and meet a familiar flower, bend down and be able to say, "I know you! Back home we have many of your relatives!"

Ann Mendershausen

1 COYOTE TOBACCO   p. 106   2 THIMBLEBERRY   p. 130

3 MATILIJA POPPY   p. 125   4 JIMSON WEED   p. 113

5 WATERFALL BUTTERCUP   p. 102   6 MARSH MARIGOLD   p. 118

7 WHITEWHORL LUPINE   p. 117   8 STICKY CINQUEFOIL   p. 104

9 MARIPOSA LILY   p. 115   10 WILD STRAWBERRY   p. 129

11 DUSKY HORKELIA   p. 112   12 BEDSTRAW   p. 99

13 GRASS-OF-PARNASSUS   p. 111   14 GAYOPHYTUM   p. 110

15 ALPINE GENTIAN   p. 110   16 BITTERROOT   p. 100

17 SPREADING PHLOX   p. 124   18 PEREGRINE THISTLE   p. 130

19 DAISY FLEABANE   p. 106   20 COULTER'S DAISY   p. 106

21 DRUMMOND'S THISTLE   p. 130   22 WHITE CLOVER   p. 104

23 WHITE HEATHER   p. 112   24 GLOBE LILY   p. 114

25 COVILLE'S COLUMBINE   p. 105   26 WASHINGTON LILY   p. 115

27 PHANTOM ORCHID   p. 121   28 MOUNTAIN LADY'S SLIPPER   p. 120

29 MACLOSKEY'S VIOLET   p. 131   30 ALUMROOT   p. 98

31 FALSE SOLOMON'S SEAL   p. 108   32 WHITESTEM HEDGE NETTLE   p. 112

33 WRIGHT'S BUCKWHEAT p. 102   34 TINCTURE PLANT p. 131

35 ROSY BUCKWHEAT p. 102   36 NUDE BUCKWHEAT p. 102

37 CORN LILY   p. 114   38 WOODLAND STAR   p. 132

39 HOODED LADIES TRESSES   p. 113   40 SIERRA REIN ORCHID   p. 122

41 ROSY EVERLASTING   p. 126   42 YARROW   p. 132

43 DEATH CAMAS   p. 106   44 BISTORT   p. 100

45 YAMPAH p. 132　46 ANGELICA p. 98

47 COW PARSNIP p. 105　48 RANGER BUTTONS p. 125

49 PACIFIC DOGWOOD   p. 107   50 LABRADOR TEA   p. 113

51 PEARLY EVERLASTING   p. 122   52 INDIAN HEMP   p.112

53 MOCK ORANGE p. 119   54 CREEK DOGWOOD p. 107

5-11-97 on 140 to Yos.

55 WESTERN AZALEA p. 99   56 DEER BRUSH p. 107

57 ALPINE WILLOW   p. 132   58 PARISH'S SNOWBERRY   p. 128

59 CALIFORNIA BUCKEYE   p. 102   60 BLUE ELDERBERRY   p. 108

61 INDIAN RHUBARB   p. 126   62 EVENING PRIMROSE   p. 125

63 CINQUEFOIL   p. 103   64 MOTH MULLEIN   p. 120

65 ALPINE GOLD BRODIAEA   p. 101   66 LEMMON'S DRABA   p. 107

67 GOLDEN BRODIAEA   p. 102   68 TOWER MUSTARD   p. 121

69 KLAMATH WEED   p. 113   70 TINKERS PENNY   p. 131

71 ST. JOHN'S WORT   p. 129   72 BLAZING STAR   p. 100

73 GREENLEAF RAILLARDELLA   p. 125   74 GIANT BLAZING STAR   p. 100

75 PALE AGOSERIS   p. 98   76 YELLOW STAR THISTLE   p. 131

77 HEARTLEAF ARNICA p. 98   78 COMMON DANDELION p. 106

79 SIERRA ARNICA p. 99   80 NODDING MICROSERIS p. 118

81 COMMON SUNFLOWER   p. 130   82 COMMON MADIA   p. 117

83 WOOLLY SUNFLOWER   p. 130   84 BIGELOW'S SNEEZEWEED   p. 128

85 BLACK-EYED SUSAN   p. 100   86 ALPINE GOLD   p. 98

87 MULE EARS   p. 120   88 CONEFLOWER   p. 105

89 WOOLLY MULLEIN   p. 121   90 NARROW GOLDENROD   p. 111

91 SIERRA WALLFLOWER   p. 132   92 WESTERN WALLFLOWER   p. 132

93 ALPINE GOLDENROD   p. 111   94 MEADOW GOLDENROD   p. 111

95 BLOOMER GOLDENBRUSH   p. 101   96 PRIMROSE MONKEY FLOWER p. 120

97 ALPINE MONKEY FLOWER   p. 119   98 SILVERLEAF LOTUS   p. 116

5-11-97 Mirror Lk. Trail

99 COMMON MONKEY FLOWER   p. 119   100 MOUNTAIN VIOLET   p. 131

101 DWARF LOUSEWORT   p. 116   102 NARROWLEAF LOTUS   p. 116

103 LOCOWEED   p. 115   104 SINGLE-STEMMED GROUNDSEL p. 111

105 SULPHUR FLOWER   p. 130   106 ALPINE BUCKWHEAT   p. 102

107 FERN-LEAVED LOMATIUM   p. 116   108 ARROWLEAF GROUNDSEL   p. 111

109 STONECROP p. 129 110 INDIAN POND LILY p. 115

111 BUSH CINQUEFOIL p. 104 112 FIDDLE NECK p. 108

113 ORANGE AGOSERIS p. 98 114 KELLY'S TIGER LILY p. 115

115 SMALL LEOPARD LILY p. 115 116 CALIFORNIA POPPY p. 124

117 FAREWELL-TO-SPRING   p. 108   118 DUDLEY'S CLARKIA   p. 104

119 WOOD ROSE   p. 126   120 SIERRA PRIMROSE   p. 125

121 CHECKERMALLOW　　　　　p. 103　　122 WILD GERANIUM　　　　　p. 110

123 SHIELDLEAF　　　　　p. 127　　124 SMOOTHSTEM FIREWEED　　　p. 109

125 ALPINE ASTER   p. 99   126 INDIAN PINK   p. 112

127 YOSEMITE ASTER   p. 99   128 WANDERING DAISY   p. 106

129 ALPINE PAINTBRUSH   p. 122   130 INDIAN PAINTBRUSH   p. 122

131 MUSTANG CLOVER   p. 121   132 LEMMON'S PAINTBRUSH   p. 122

133 PINK MONKEY FLOWER   p. 120   134 SPREADING DOGBANE   p. 107

135 CRIMSON MONKEY FLOWER   p. 119   136 LAYNE'S MONKEY FLOWER   p. 119

137 PURPLE MILKWEED   p. 118   138 SHOWY MILKWEED   p. 118

139 STEERS-HEAD   p. 129   140 WESTERN BLEEDINGHEART   p. 101

141 OWLS CLOVER   p. 122   142 CALIFORNIA FUCHSIA   p. 109

143 TOMCAT CLOVER   p. 104   144 RED CLOVER   p. 104

145 SCARLET PENSTEMON   p. 124   146 MOUNTAIN PRIDE PENSTEMON p. 124

147 LIVE-FOREVER   p. 115   148 DAVIDSON'S PENSTEMON   p. 123

149 SHOOTING STAR   p. 127   150 ALPINE SHOOTING STAR   p. 127

151 CRIMSON COLUMBINE   p. 105   152 SCARLET GILIA   p. 110

153 MOUNTAIN HEATHER p. 111   154 ALPINE LAUREL p. 114

155 DWARF BILBERRY p. 100   156 GIANT TRILLIUM p. 131

157 SHINLEAF p. 127 158 CANDYSTICK p. 103

159 SNOW PLANT p. 128 160 PINEDROPS p. 124

161 SPOTTED CORALROOT   p. 105   162 MOUNTAIN PENNYROYAL   p. 123

163 SWAMP ONION   p. 121   164 WESTERN PENNYROYAL   p. 123

165 SPIRAEA   p. 129   166 ROSEROOT   p. 126

167 FOXGLOVE   p. 109   168 CATERPILLAR PLANT   p. 103

169 FIREWEED   p. 109   170 STEPHANOMERIA   p. 129

171 BULL ELEPHANTS HEAD   p. 108   172 LITTLE ELEPHANTS HEAD   p. 108

173 GIANT HYSSOP   p. 112   174 PUSSYPAWS   p. 125

175 FIELD MINT   p. 119   176 SPEARMINT   p. 128

177 VELVETY STICKSEED   p. 129   178 SPICE BUSH   p. 128

179 MANZANITA   p. 117   180 WESTERN REDBUD   p. 126

181 WINECUP CLARKIA p. 104 182 CANCHALAGUA p. 103

183 BLUE-EYED GRASS p. 101 184 CALIFORNIA BLUEBELL p. 101

185 ROCKFRINGE   p. 126   186 BABY-BLUE EYES   p. 99

187 CAMAS LILY   p. 114   188 HIKERS GENTIAN   p. 110

189 BLUE FLAX   p. 109 190 BUSH LUPINE   p. 117

191 BLUE CURLS   p. 101 192 MONKSHOOD   p. 120

193 BROADLEAF LUPINE   p. 117   194 BREWER'S LUPINE   p. 116

195 MINIATURE LUPINE   p. 117   196 HARLEQUIN LUPINE   p. 117

197 LARKSPUR p. 113   198 TOWER LARKSPUR p. 114

199 MEADOW PENSTEMON p. 124   200 BLUE PENSTEMON p. 123

201 GRASS NUTS   p. 111   202 SIERRA LESSINGIA   p. 114

on 120 going home 5-11-97

203 ELEGANT BRODIAEA   p. 101   204 BULL THISTLE   p. 130

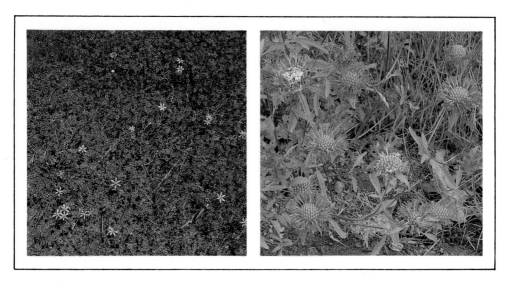

205 BRIDGE'S GILIA   p. 110   206 COYOTE MINT   p. 119

207 SKY PILOT   p. 127   208 SELFHEAL   p. 126

209 WESTERN VIOLET   p. 132   210 BLUE-EYED MARY   p. 101

211 SIERRA NEVADA PEA   p. 122   212 CHINESE PAGODAS   p. 103

213 WESTERN VERBENA   p. 131   214 FIESTA FLOWER   p. 108

215 MOUNTAIN LUNGWORT   p. 116   216 WILD IRIS   p. 113

217 MOUNTAIN SORREL   p. 128   218 MEADOW RUE   p. 118

219 WILD GINGER   p. 110   220 DAVIDSON'S FRITILLARY   p. 109

221 DEERS-TONGUE   p. 107   222 TURKEY MULLEIN   p. 120

223 CHINQUAPIN   p. 103   224 GREEN REIN ORCHID   p. 121

DESCRIPTIONS
OF THE
FLOWERS

AGOSERIS, ORANGE   *Agoseris aurantiaca*   SUNFLOWER FAMILY
                                                         pl. 113

A rare example of the SUNFLOWER FAMILY that is orange! It closely resembles a **Dandelion** except it can be taller (up to 20 inches). The blossoms consist entirely of ray flowers (no disk flowers). Leaves are spatula-shaped and basal at the stem. It grows in dry meadows and open forests, especially around upper Crane Flat. Middle elevations. June to August.

AGOSERIS, PALE   *Agoseris glauca*   SUNFLOWER FAMILY
                                                   pl. 75

It is similar to the **Orange Agoseries** *(A. aurantiaca),* which are **Dandelion** look-alikes, except the ray flowers are yellow and less numerous than on the **Dandelion.** The flower heads are on a single stem up to 20 inches tall with spatula-shaped, basal leaves. Found in dry forests and dry open meadows. June to August.

ALPINE, GOLD   *Hulsea algida*   SUNFLOWER FAMILY
                                               pl. 86

This is the loftiest of all SUNFLOWERS, rarely growing below 10,000-feet. What a delightful treat when first spotted after much steep and exposed hiking! It will seek open, sandy areas above timberline and will send out comparatively long (4- to 16-inch) stems in defiance of the constant alpine summer winds. The yellow disk flowers are surrounded by 25 to 50 ray flowers. The leaves are sticky, hairy, pinnate, and clustered on the ground. Named after an army surgeon, Gilbert Hulse; *algida* means "gold." August to September.

ALUMROOT   *Heuchera micrantha*   SAXIFRAGE FAMILY
                    var. erubescens   **pl. 30**

This species of **Alumroot** grows at lower elevations (2,500- to 7,000-feet) than its cousin, *H. rubescens,* but both are similar. The blossoms are tiny, white, bell-shaped flowers clustered at the end of 12- to 24-inch stems. The leaves are maple-shaped, grouped at the woody base. This is a perennial that regenerates each spring from a hardy rootstock. In fall, the leaves turn a striking crimson before dying back for a winter nap. It prefers rocky cliffs and ledges and usually can be found along the upper portion of the Four-Mile Trail. It is also prevalent in the Merced Canyon. *Heuchera* was named after Johann Heucher, a German medical botanist; *micrantha* means "minute flowers." The roots have an alum-like taste, hence the common name. Indians used the powdered roots as a poultice to treat sores. May to July.

ANGELICA   *Angelica lineariloba*   CARROT FAMILY
                                                  pl. 46

This tall (2- to 6-foot) perennial grows along meadow fringes or moist roadside areas. The flowers are actually a cluster of many tiny flowers displayed in an umbrella shape up to 6-inches across. The leaves are broad, toothed, and most often appear to be fuzzy. 4,000- to 8,000-feet. Latin *Angelica* referred to its medicinal properties. June to August.

ARNICA, HEARTLEAF   *Arnica cordifolia*   SUNFLOWER FAMILY
                                                       pl. 77

A yellow Sunflower-like blossom with 9 to 14 ray flowers surrounding a compact head of tiny disk flowers. Stems are 8- to 24-inches high with several pairs of heart-shaped leaves. Stems and

98

leaves are woolly. It is usually found growing in shaded woodlands, clustered in groups, from 4,000- to 10,000-feet. All **Arnicas** have opposite leaves and a distinctive odor. They are medicinal plants, the oil of which continues to be used for sprains and bruises. May to August.

ARNICA, SIERRA *Arnica nevadensis* SUNFLOWER FAMILY
pl. 79

This plant is very similar to the **Heartleaf Arnica** except the leaves are more oblong and the ray tips are three-toothed instead of pointed. It grows 4- to 12-inches high along streambanks and moist seeps at higher elevations. July to August.

ASTER, ALPINE *Aster alpigenus* SUNFLOWER FAMILY
pl. 125

This flower has pink-to-purple ray flowers and contrasting yellow disk flowers. The blossoms sit atop a short (2- to 16-inch) stem that is at first prostrate and then rises as the plant matures. The leaves are grass-like and basal; it grows in mountain meadows 6,000- to 10,000-feet. *Aster* means "star" and *alpigenus* means "alpine." June to September.

ASTER, YOSEMITE *Aster occidentalis* SUNFLOWER FAMILY
var. *yosemitanus* pl. 127

This is "Yosemite's star!" — A variety common to drying meadow fringes and forest floors from 4,000- to 7,000-feet. The blossom has 20 to 35 purple ray flowers around yellow disk flowers. The 12- to 24-inch stem is multibranched near the top, each branch having a blossom at its tip. The leaves are slender and lancelike. *Aster* means "star," *occidentalis* means "western" and of course *yosemitanus* "of Yosemite." This species was first collected in 1877 near Vernal Fall by Joseph Hooker and Asa Gray. Dr. Gray, a professor at Harvard University, played an important part in the identification of many Sierra wildflowers. There are numerous mentions of specimens from Yosemite being sent to him for identification. He is also noted for coordinating early American and European botanical studies. It blooms July to September.

AZALEA, WESTERN *Rhododendron* HEATH FAMILY
occidentale pl. 55

This deep-green shrub will dominate the landscape of Yosemite Valley during the month of June, and the stunning white clusters of tubular blossoms will perk up your saunters around the valley floor. Its flower is 1- to 2-inches long (length of the fused part of the corolla), and has a five-lobed star shape, with the top lobe splashed by a bit of yellow. After pollination by the Hawkmoth, the yellow fades. It can grow up to 10-feet tall. As the **Dogwood's** white bracts wane, the **Azalea** assumes the task of adorning the shorebanks of the now full Merced River. June to July.

BABY-BLUE EYES *Nemophila menziesii* WATERLEAF FAMILY
pl. 186

Individually, this delicate beauty would be an insignificant part of the foothill landscape, but it seems to congregate into impressive blue pools that can be spotted from great distances. The blossoms gather so close that the 4- to 10-inch hairy stems and compound, deeply divided leaves are rarely observed. Each tiny flower is a five-petaled cup with blue fringes and a white center. It grows on the grassy slopes from 2,000- to 4,000-feet. *Nemophila* means "grove loving" and *menziesii* is named after Scottish naturalist Archibald Menzies. March to May.

BEDSTRAW *Galium aparine* BEDSTRAW FAMILY
pl. 12

Introduced from Europe, this striking creeper will be found spreading in Yosemite's shaded areas. The hairy, four-sided stem has whorled leaves that are also hairy. These leaf hairs enable the plant to cling and climb over other vegetation. It will grow 1- to 5-feet long and appear to be like a vine lying on the ground. One place to locate this common plant is in the **Cattail** bog east of Gates of The Valley on Northside Drive. *Galium* means "milk," the Indians used to make a cooling drink to reduce fevers from a close cousin of this plant, **Fragrant Bedstraw** *(G. triflorum)*. The common name **"Bedstraw"** comes from early settlers using this plant to stuff mattresses. April to July.

BILBERRY, DWARF   *Vaccinium nivictum*   HEATH FAMILY
                                                          pl. 155

This little guy truly suffers an identity crisis! It is quite common but rarely observed by hikers. Once seen and recognized you will continue to marvel at its diminutive beauty each time you spot it along the high meadows and trails. The flowers are bell- or urn-shaped, the leaves are oval and alternate, forming a 2- to 4-inch high matted ground cover. Its real glory comes later in the season, for when meadow grasses begin to turn brown, its leaves shine crimson. *Vaccinium* is Latin for **"Bilberry."** Flowers June to July. Berries appear in August.

BISTORT   *Polygonum bistortoides*   BUCKWHEAT FAMILY
                                                       pl. 44

A common and obvious member of the wet meadow community, the **Bistort** blossom is actually a cone-shaped cluster of tiny flowers up to 2-inches long. The leaves are 4- to 10-inches long, broad and lancelike, and are usually hidden in the lush meadow grasses that compete for the high nourishment of the moist soil. The Sierra variety is unique from its eastern cousins, reproducing itself from hardy rootstocks instead of seeds. The name *Polygonum* means "many jointed" and *bistort* means "twice twisted." June to August.

BITTERROOT, YOSEMITE   *Lewisia disepala*   PURSLANE FAMILY
                                                             pl. 16

This lovely *Lewisia* is considered to be endemic to Yosemite. It has the large 2- to 3-inch pink blossoms of *L. ridiviva*, but it only has two-sepals that are fairly obvious. The obscure leaves are tufted, fleshy, linear and tucked neatly under the large blossoms. It can be found on the gravelly, sandy ground around Yosemite's rim area, such as Olmsted Point. June to July.

BLACK-EYED SUSAN   *Rudbeckia hirta*   SUNFLOWER FAMILY
                                                        pl. 85

A close cousin to the **Coneflower,** this non-native can be found widely scattered where early pioneer settlements were located. It has individual yellow ray flowers meeting at a dark brown or black center, which is actually many individual disk flowers. It has 2- to 3-inch blossoms on stems 2- to 4-feet high. The leaves are lancelike and hairy. Found throughout most of the meadows of Yosemite Valley. *Rudbeckia* means "most hairy." July to August.

BLAZING STAR   *Mentzelia lindleyi*   LOASA FAMILY
                          ssp. *crocea*   **pl. 72**

This **Blazing Star** blooms late in the season for low elevation flowers. You can see the bright golden yellow of **Blazing Stars** around El Portal and one patch about a mile down on the Hite's Cove Trail, on the South Fork of the Merced River. The 2- to 3-inch blossom has five nearly oval petals which sit on top of a 6-inch to 3-foot tall stem. The leaves are **Dandelion-like,** up to 6-inches long and arranged alternately. It prefers dry soil on open flats below 4,000-feet. *Mentzelia* is named after a seventeenth century German botanist, C. Mentzel. March to June.

BLAZING STAR, GIANT   *Mentzelia laevicaulis*   LOASA FAMILY
                                                                 pl. 74

This cousin to **Lindley's Blazing Star** can be found on either side of the Sierra crest, growing up to 8,000-feet. It is a tall (2- to 4-foot) plant and the five-petals are lancelike and pointed. The leaves are triangular and sharply toothed. It, too, prefers dry rocky soil and lots of sun. The most likely place to find this flower is east of the Tioga Pass on Highway 120. June to October.

BLEEDINGHEART,　　　*Dicentra formosa*　　　BLEEDINGHEART FAMILY
WESTERN　　　　　　　　　　　　　　　　　**pl. 140**

Nature has so many wonderful surprises for those who explore! Both the leaves and flowers of this plant show off her talents. The leaves are pinnate, ¾- to 2-inches long and appear as a bluish kelly-green, elaborately soft and lacy. The flowers are a delightful, four-petaled, billowy sack in the shape of a pink heart, snuggled in this 8- to 18-inch tall plant. Often seen around the base of Bridalveil Fall. *Dicentra* means "two spurred" and *formosa* means "beautiful." March to July.

BLOOMER GOLDENBRUSH　　*Haplopappus bloomeri*　　SUNFLOWER FAMILY
　　　　　　　　　　　　　　　　　　　　　　　　pl. 95

These blossoms never seem to quite open, always looking like the blossom will reach maturity in just a few days. It resembles a shrub more than a bush and can be found lining the roads, like a hedge. Approximately 2-feet tall. The yellow flowering heads appear at the end of one to five stems. The leaves are narrow and linear. July to September.

BLUE CURLS　　　　　　*Trichostema*　　　　　MINT FAMILY
　　　　　　　　　　　　　lanceolatum　　　　　**pl. 191**

This is a puzzling find when first encountered, for it looks like a cross between a **Steers Head** and an **Elephants Head** twisted backward. Both familiar-looking and all wrong at the same time. This unique plant has a blossom that is five-petaled, tubular and twisted so that the stamen points back toward the stem, like a scorpion's uplifted tail. Its lancelike, hairy leaves are opposite, arranged on a 4- to 24-inch stem, and exude a strong odor. Grows in dry, open places. *Trichos* means "hair," *stema* "stamen," and *lanceolatum* "lance-leaved." July to October.

BLUEBELL, CALIFORNIA　　*Campanula*　　　　BLUEBELL FAMILY
　　　　　　　　　　　　　　prenanthoides　　　**pl. 184**

This light blue, 1- to 1½-inch, delicate flower sits erect on a simple 10- to 20-inch stem. When the flowers mature they will have five back-curled petals and a baseball-bat-shaped pistil protruding far past the blossom. The leaves are lancelike, toothed and mostly grouped on the bottom half of the stem. It prefers moist, open pine forests from 3,000- to 6,000-feet. June to September.

BLUE-EYED GRASS　　　*Sisyrinchium bellum*　　IRIS FAMILY
　　　　　　　　　　　　　　　　　　　　　　　　pl. 183

This is a grass-like plant that blooms most of the summer. The 6- to 24-inch stem rises from the lancelike leaves and bears a small, delicate, six-petaled, purple blossom with a yellow center. The contrasting colors attract bees to its nectar and the plant is thus pollinated. It grows each year from a hardy, stringy rootstock in moist mountain meadows. *Sisyrinchium* is a Greek word for an unknown **Iris** and the Latin name *bellum* means "beautiful." The Indians used the roots for a laxative. March to July.

BLUE-EYED MARY　　　*Collinsia torreyi*　　　FIGWORT FAMILY
　　　　　　　　　　　　　　　　　　　　　　　　pl. 210

This is one member of the *Collinsia* genus that does not grow in symmetrical whorls. Instead, the plant features delicate little two-lipped blossoms. The upper lip is pale or white and the lower lip royal blue. The blossoms are small but grow in masses and are attention-getters when at their prime. Leaves are lancelike on stems up to 24-inches tall. *Collinsia* is named after Zacchaus Collins, a botanist from Philadelphia, and *torreyi* commemorates a famous American Botanist, Dr. John Torrey. May to July.

BRODIAEA, ALPINE GOLD　*Brodiaea gracilis*　　AMARYLLIS FAMILY
　　　　　　　　　　　　　　var. *analina*　　　　**pl. 67**

A smaller, daintier version of **Golden Brodiaea** *(B. lutea)* usually found at higher elevations on open flats or in dry forests. Brown mid-ribs are hidden on the underside of the blossom. *Brodiaea* means "little beauty" and *gracilis* means "slender." May to August.

BRODIAEA, ELEGANT　　　*Brodiaea elegans*　　AMARYLLIS FAMILY
　　　　　　　　　　　　　　　　　　　　　　　　pl. 203

This funnel-shaped blue flower clusters as an umbrella atop a single 4- to 16-inch stem. Leaves are linear and basal but usually wither by flowering time. They can be found from 2,000- to

7,000-feet, on grassy hillsides or drying meadows in early summer. *Brodiaea* is named after the Scottish botanist James Brodie; and *elegans* means "elegant." May to July.

| **BRODIAEA, GOLDEN** | *Brodiaea lutea* | AMARYLLIS FAMILY |
| | var. *scabra* | **pl. 65** |

This eye-catching yellow-gold flower is a six-petaled, symmetrically shaped blossom that grows 8- to 32-inches tall on multiple stems. The petals have delicate, brown rib markings. It grows around El Portal and the lower Merced River, covering large areas with the appearance of golden stars sprinkled liberally about. *Lutea* means "yellow." April to July.

| **BUCKEYE, CALIFORNIA** | *Aesculus californica* | BUCKEYE FAMILY |
| | | **pl. 59** |

This is another of the spectacular plants-for-all-seasons that inhabit the Park. Early spring finds the palm shaped, compound (five to seven leaflets) leaves of this shrub-like tree bright green. May and June bring creamy white candles or spikes of flowers to light it up. In the late summer the leaves dry and fall off revealing large, brown nuts or seeds. The nuts are poisonous and were pulverized by the Indians and dispersed in the water to aid their fishing efforts. It can be seen from the Arch Rock Entrance Station to El Portal on Highway 140.

| **BUCKWHEAT, ALPINE** | *Eriogonum ovalifolium* | BUCKWHEAT FAMILY |
| | | **pl. 106** |

In Yosemite this variety is usually found above timberline and is often called **"Oval-leafed Buckwheat."** Its blossoms, like others in this family, are umbrella-like clusters of flowers. It will start as creamy yellow and turn to a stunning burgundy as the season progresses. The ½-inch leaves are silvery gray and form a dense mat in the windswept alpine country. *Eriogonum* means "woolly joints" and *ovalifolium* means "oval-leaved." July to August.

| **BUCKWHEAT, NUDE** | *Eriogonum nudum* | BUCKWHEAT FAMILY |
| | | **pl. 36** |

This BUCKWHEAT was so named because the 12- to 36-inch stems appear stark naked, adorned only with lovely ¾-inch white or pink clusters of tiny flowers at the tips. Its leaves will be found whorled at the base, lying flat on the ground. This species is at home in all elevations, from the foothills to timberline, and inhabits roadsides and open forests with well-drained, sandy soil. May to December.

| **BUCKWHEAT, ROSY** | *Eriogonum roseum* | BUCKWHEAT FAMILY |
| | | **pl. 35** |

This very plain BUCKWHEAT is rarely the center of attention, but it is always found playing a supporting role to the more showy stars of the neighborhood. It grows on an erect, branchless stem, 12- to 24-inches high. Each blossom is a cluster of tiny pom-pom-like flowers bundled tightly together, clasping the stem at regular intervals. The leaves are basal and oblong. Look for it on dry, sandy flats or meadow fringes below 5,000-feet. June to October.

| **BUCKWHEAT, WRIGHT'S** | *Eriogonum wrightii* | BUCKWHEAT FAMILY |
| | | **pl. 33** |

Wright's Buckwheat is a later bloomer than most. A good place to see it is along the Tioga Road in dry, rocky places. From a moving vehicle it appears as a mass of dry sage; but when you stop to examine it more closely, you begin to appreciate its delicate white and pink flowers, tightly clustered along a stem that most often is prostrate from its own weight. The stems rise out of a thick, woody tuft of lancelike leaves, making the plant 12- to 18-inches in diameter. The stems are usually twice as high as the leaf tuft. July to September.

| **BUTTERCUP, WATERFALL** | *Ranunculus hystriculus* | BUTTERCUP FAMILY |
| | | **pl. 5** |

This delicate, five-petaled creamy blossom can be found growing on mossy rock ledges and in moist places around waterfalls. The stems are 6- to 18-inches long, with maple-shaped leaves. It grows at lower elevations 3,000- to 6,000-feet. *Ranunculus* is Latin for "little frog" (frogs are in its habitat). April to June.

CANCHALAGUA   *Centaurium venustum*   GENTIAN FAMILY
pl. 182

This charming little meadow flower is often overlooked because of the taller grasses it communes with. You can look for it on the fringes of west El Capitan Meadow. Growing only 4- to 12-inches high on fragile but resistant stems. The leaves are oval-shaped and opposite. The blossoms are five-petaled stars that flare from a tube. The entire blossom is only ¾″ wide. The name *Centaurium* comes from Greek Mythology, the half-horse/half-man, Centaur Chiron, who was said to have discovered medicinal properties in this plant. *Venustum* relates to the beautiful Greek Goddess Venus, because the plant is so beautiful. The Indians and the Spanish used this plant to make a fever-reducing tea, hence the Spanish name, **Canchalagua.** June to August.

CANDYSTICK   *Allotropa virgata*   WINTERGREEN FAMILY
pl. 158

This is a non-chlorophyll-bearing plant and exists by a mycorrhizal relationship (see **Pinedrops**). The **Candystick** is less common than its cousin, **Pinedrops,** but much more spectacular. It stands 8- to 24-inches tall and appears to be a giant red striped peppermint stick. The flowers are urn-like white blossoms with protruding red stamens. Adaptation has reduced the leaves to scales along the stem. Instead of using photosynthesis, it derives its nourishment from fungi that grow in the thick decaying humus of the forest floor. June to August.

CATERPILLAR PLANT   *Phacelia mutabilis*   WATERLEAF FAMILY
pl. 168

The first sight of this plant makes the reason for the common name quite obvious, for the stems appear to be crawling with woolly caterpillars. The blossoms are actually tiny clusters of ¼-inch flowers at the end of small stemlets which curl under themselves. The stamens protrude upward, giving them the appearance of long, bristly hairs. Leaves are gray, linear and basal. The entire plant stands 8- to 24-inches tall and can be found on dry flats from 2,000- to 8,000-feet. *Phacelia* means "clustered" and *mutabilis* means "varied" (colors range from green to yellow to lavender). June to August.

CHECKERMALLOW   *Sidalcea glaucescens*   MALLOW FAMILY
pl. 121

This dainty pink member of the MALLOW clan is a delightful addition to dry, open meadow and grassland areas. The five-petaled 1-inch blossoms are loosely arranged on a stem 12- to 24-inches tall. The leaves are deeply lobed with five to seven divisions. It grows at elevations from 3,000- to 11,000-feet. At one time the Mallow's thick sap was used in the production of marshmallows. Today different ingredients are used to produce this same confection. Early settlers used the leaves to make a poultice for stings and infections. May to July.

CHINESE PAGODAS   *Collinsia heterophylla*   FIGWORT FAMILY
pl. 212

The overall appearance of this unique wildflower reminds you of a Chinese pagoda. The blossoms are in whorled tiers stacked in a pyramidal configuration. Each individual blossom is two-lipped, the lower being the longest and ranging in color from pink to purple. The upper lip is lighter in color and smaller. The stems are 8- to 20-inches tall with lancelike and opposite leaves. They are usually found growing in shade around El Portal and the along Hite's Cove trail, in dry, sandy soil. March to June.

CHINQUAPIN   *Castanopsis*   BEECH FAMILY
sempervirens   pl. 223

This shrub is an evergreen, a regal inhabitant of dry, rocky slopes, where it can be found mingling with the equally impressive **Manzanita.** It is usually not noticed while flowering, but soon develops a stunning amber burr, that ripens during September and October. The 3-inch leaves are oblong and bi-colored, green on top, yellow-gold underneath. It can be found growing up to 6-feet tall along Highway 41 between Chinquapin (named for the abundance of this plant) and Wawona.

CINQUEFOIL   *Potentilla gracilis*   ROSE FAMILY
pl. 63

The brilliant yellow five-petaled flowers have five distinguishing alternate green sepals underneath. However the name prefix *(Cinque)* refers to the five to seven fingerlike leaflets *(foil),* not the petals. It grows 15- to 30-inches high at varied elevations from Yosemite Valley to timberline. It likes moist meadows and streambanks and will frequent all of them. June to August.

| CINQUEFOIL, BUSH | *Potentilla fruticosa* | ROSE FAMILY |
| | | pl. 111 |

This variety of **Cinquefoil** also has yellow, rose-like flowers, but stands on top of a shrub with a multibranched stem 12- to 48-inches tall. The leaves are deeply cut in three to seven leaflets. It favors the moist, rocky areas of the subalpine region. *Potentilla* means "somewhat potent" (medicinally) and *fruticosa* means "having fruit." June to July.

| CINQUEFOIL, STICKY | *Potentilla glanulosa* | ROSE FAMILY |
| | | pl. 8 |

This **Cinquefoil** is creamy-white to pale yellow instead of the more common bright yellow of the other species. It can grow tall (up to 30-inches) and likes almost all growing conditions as long as it has ample light. The leaves are divided and multi-lobed with toothed fringes and a sticky stem. It will usually be found below 10,000-feet. *Potentilla* means "potent" (medicinally). It was used as a cure for colds and stomach aches and also as a tonic for infections. *Glanulosa* means "having glands," *cinque,* "five" and *foil,* "leaves." May to August.

| CLARKIA, DUDLEY'S | *Clarkia dudleyana* | EVENING PRIMROSE FAMILY |
| | | pl. 118 |

This pink **Clarkia** is almost identical to **Farewell-To-Spring** *(C. williamsonii)* except that it has no dark spots. Its petals are white-ribbed and the buds droop downward. It prefers dry slopes and fields below 5,000-feet. *Clarkia* is named after William Clark, leader of the Lewis and Clark expedition, and *dudleyana* is named after the botanist William Dudley. The Indians who lived in the foothills enjoyed eating the seeds of this lovely plant. May to July.

| CLARKIA, WINECUP | *Clarkia purpurea* | EVENING PRIMROSE FAMILY |
| | | pl. 181 |

This **Clarkia** is less common than the others in the Park, but you can find this beauty in the meadow at Devil's Elbow along Northside Drive. It is four-petaled, royal blue or purple, and each petal has a spot in its center. The leaves are linear, the buds erect. It grows 6- to 12-inches high. *Clarkia* is named after William Clark, of the Lewis and Clark expedition, and *purpurea* means "purple." May to July.

| CLOVER, RED | *Trifolium pratense* | PEA FAMILY |
| | | pl. 144 |

The blossom is the key to this plant — a cluster of pea-like flowers mostly a reddish-purple, forming a large pom-pom that sits atop a 6- to 12-inch stem. The leaves are tri-lobed, with each lobe having a white chevron (>) in the center. There is "no" bract (a leaf often mistaken for a flower petal) under the blossom in this species. It likes moist places; good examples are in the seeps along Highway 120 between Crane Flat and the first tunnel (toward the Valley). *Trifolium* means "three-leaved." April to July.

| CLOVER, TOMCAT | *Trifolium tridentatum* | PEA FAMILY |
| | | pl. 143 |

This **Clover** has a flower head of tightly clustered, pea-shaped blossoms that are pink with white tips. The tri-lobed leaves *(Trifolium)* are lancelike and sharply toothed. Each sepal has three-sharp points that appear as spikes whorled around the stem. It grows 5-to 24-inches tall and likes moist areas to 5,000-feet. Found in the grasslands of Yosemite Valley. March to July.

| CLOVER, WHITE | *Trifolium repens* | PEA FAMILY |
| | | pl. 22 |

A white pom-pom blossom usually ¾ inch in diameter made up of tightly clustered pea-shaped flowers (irregular five-petaled blossoms with the upper lip dominating). The leaves are palm-shaped and three-lobed. It can be found commonly in meadows throughout Yosemite Valley. April to October.

COLUMBINE, COVILLE'S   *Aquilegia pubescens*   BUTTERCUP FAMILY
pl. 25

This stunning white flower is five-petaled with spurs. The contrasting pale yellow stamens protrude beyond the blossom but are not as pronounced as in *Aquilegia formosa.* Cross hybridization occurs when the Hawkmoth, which is the exclusive pollinator of *A. formosa,* happens to land on the *A. pubescens'* protruding stamens. The Hummingbird with its long beak, also plays a role as pollinator for the *A. pubescens,* carrying the pollen from plant to plant. The blossoms are larger in *A. pubescens* (1½-inches across) and will readily hybridize, so the color can vary from the predominant creamy-white to pink, yellow or lavender from the resulting cross-pollinated seeds. Blossoms are erect on stems up to 24-inches high. It is found in rock crevices above timberline. Columbine comes from the French word *columbe,* a dove. The shape of the petals suggest five doves perched around a fountain. *Aquila* means "eagle" (the spurs look like an eagles claw); *pubescens* means "with fine short hairs." June to August.

COLUMBINE, CRIMSON   *Aquilegia formosa*   BUTTERCUP FAMILY
pl. 151

The **Crimson Columbine** is truly a delight to discover while walking through woods from 4,000- to 8,000-feet. They also refresh you on the trail to Nevada Fall, under the seeping rock walls as you reach the end of your journey. There are five long, red petals that form spurs at the back and curl outward on the front. Its bright yellow pistils protrude beyond the petals, offering a colorful contrast and also helping the Hawkmoth pollinate. The entire blossom hangs downward from long (24- to 48-inch) stems. The leaves are low on the stem and tri-lobed. It is found along seeps and mountain streams. *Aquila* means "eagle" (the spurs remind you of an eagle's claw); *formosa* means "beautiful." April to August.

CONEFLOWER   *Rudbeckia californica*   SUNFLOWER FAMILY
pl. 88

This is a unique member of the SUNFLOWER FAMILY. Its 2- to 3-inch ray flowers are yellow and usually droop downward. In the center is a multitude of brown disk flowers standing 1- to 2-inch high in a distinctive cone shape. The blossoms stand above other members of the community on a stout stem from 3 to 6 feet high. The leaves are broadly lancelike. During late June and July the areas around Crane Flat sparkle with the vibrant yellow of **Coneflowers** waving in the gentle summer breeze — a truly worthwhile show to watch! They are also found around Chinquapin on Highway 41. Named after the botanist Olaf Rudbeck, who first identified the species and of course, *californica,* after the state where it is most prevalent. June to August.

CORALROOT, SPOTTED   *Corallorhiza maculata*   ORCHID FAMILY
pl. 161

The **Spotted Coralroot, Phantom Orchid,** and **Striped Coralroot** are three of the few plants that have a mycorrhizal relationship outside the WINTERGREEN FAMILY (see **Pinedrops**). The **Spotted Coralroot** most often can be found beneath the humus-producing conifers. Its blossoms are Orchid-shaped and orange-red in color, with the lower three-lobes forming the white and purple spotted lower lip. Each 6- to 30-inch stem will have 12 to 15 flowers, and leaves that have adapted to mere papery scales. The root system is the source of the plant's common name. The myriad of multibranched and spreading tentacles resemble a hardy sea coral. It blooms in July and August after which the fruit appears as red-to-brown nodding pods. It will stand all winter as a monument to its past beauty and a suggestion of the splendor to come. June to August.

COW PARSNIP   *Heracleum lanatum*   CARROT FAMILY
pl. 47

Everything about this wildflower is proportionately gigantic. It stands up to 12-feet tall on a stout stalk. The flowers can be 12-inches wide, consisting of 15 to 30 smaller umbels. The entire grouping resembles white lacework. The leaves are up to 12-inches wide and maple-shaped. Its overall scale does justice to the size of Yosemite Valley's cliffs and waterfalls. It likes wet meadows up to 8,000 feet. Because of its great size, the Yosemite Indians were able to use this plant for food by peeling the stalk and cooking the tender center. It was named after the Greek God Hercules long before the new-world genus name, *Uncumboreal* was given. Hercules was said to give this plant as medicine to his men in battle. *Lanatum* means "woolly." April to August.

COYOTE TOBACCO *Nicotiana acuminata* NIGHTSHADE FAMILY
  var. multiflora **pl. 1**

This typical NIGHTSHADE has a tubular, five-petaled, white blossom that appears to be a trumpet announcing the arrival of a monarch. The beauty of its horn-shaped flower is all that it has going for it, for it is a flower people love to hate. Even its common name (Coyote) implies disdain, for legend suggests the Coyote represents evil. The 1- to 2-foot stems and the oval, pointed leaves are quite sticky and exude a repulsive odor. Many Indians used this plant as a smoking material, so *Nicotiana* was named after Jean Nicot, a French diplomat, who introduced tobacco from Portugal to France in 1561. This plant is native to South America. The species name *acuminata* means "pointed leaves." It can be found growing on dry flats from 2,500- to 5,000-feet. Look for it across from the Chapel on the meadow fringe. July to September.

DAISY, COULTER'S *Erigeron coulteri* SUNFLOWER FAMILY
  pl. 20

Even though this white **Daisy** is not common, it will be easily spotted, for it grows in a predominantly green environment of wet meadows and lush streambanks. Its tall (1- to 4-feet) stem has lancelike, clasping leaves. The 50-plus white ray flowers encircle a yellow disk flower, with only one blossom per stem. It grows at elevations of 3,000- to 8,000-feet. The name means *Eri* "early" (blooming) and *geron* "old man." Named after botanist John Merle Coulter. June to August.

DAISY FLEABANE *Erigeron strigosus* SUNFLOWER FAMILY
  pl. 19

This is a distinctive member of a very confusing tribe. It is easy to become bewildered by all the different **Asters, Daisies** and **Fleabanes** in the Park, so finding this one will be refreshing. The blossoms are much smaller (½- to 1-inch wide), it has 50 to 100 white ray flowers around yellow disk flowers. The plant is tall (1½- to 4-feet) and multibranched near the flowering heads. The leaves are spatula-shaped and bristly. The common name is derived from "days eye" because the flower only opens during the daylight. It is a transplant from the east coast and was brought out by early settlers who packed their linen and clothes with the dried flowers to keep the fleas out, hence the name **"Fleabane"** (flea killer). The Latin name *Eri* means "early" (blooming), *geron* "old man" and *strigosus* "bristly." June to August.

DAISY, WANDERING *Erigeron peregrinus* SUNFLOWER FAMILY
  pl. 128

This **Daisy** is the most common variety found in Yosemite. The blossom has many purple ray flowers around yellow disk flowers. They sit atop a spindly 4- to 20-inch stem and can be found in forests and meadows from 4,000- to 9,000-feet. *Eri* means "early" (blooming) and *peregrinus* means "wandering" (as in Peregrine Falcons). July to September.

DANDELION, COMMON *Taraxacum officinale* SUNFLOWER FAMILY
  pl. 78

A primary example of the dual role flowers play in our lives. At home, Park visitors spend many dollars and hours each year to eradicate the **Dandelion** from lawns and gardens, then come to Yosemite and admire it as a wildflower. The flower (¾- to 1-inch wide) is made up of many yellow ray flowers and has no center disk flowers. The leaves are 2- to 16-inches long, lancelike, deeply cut, with back-pointing teeth. The flower turns to a delicate puffball made up of seeds and hairlike wings that enable the seeds to be dispersed by the summer winds. It is one of the few weeds found in Tuolumne Meadows, with an ever-increasing patch near the road to Soda Springs. April to August.

DEATH CAMAS *Zigadenus venenosus* LILY FAMILY
  pl. 43

This also is a member of moist meadow communities, typically found growing with **Camas Lilies, Bistorts, Shooting Stars** and **Swamp Onions.** Because it is equally as beautiful and strikingly similar to the **Swamp Onion,** it is often perceived to be as harmless. "Caution," all parts of this plant are highly toxic to both animals and humans. It has been known to quickly kill grazing livestock. The flower is a terminal spike at the end of a 12- to 20-inch stout stalk. Each flower is six-petaled, with the inner three being slightly shorter and the stamens longer than the petals. The leaves are long, strap-like and appear to grow from a common point. As with the **Camas Lily**, it grows from a bulb, this one having a black sheath surrounding it. May to July.

| **DEER BRUSH** | *Ceanothus integerrimus* | BUCKTHORN FAMILY |
| | | pl. 56 |

Deer Brush is a shrub that is most prized by browsing deer. It will grow from 4- to 12-feet high, displaying many white blossoms clustered at the end of its branches. The leaves are 2-inches long and oval-shaped. The flower's cluster can be used as a soap: just add water and scrub. A lather forms and your hands are clean. It grows in forest openings and exposed slopes at low-to-moderate elevations and is very evident along Highway 140 from El Portal to the Arch Rock Entrance Station in early summer. April to July.

| **DEERS-TONGUE** | *Frasera speciosa* | GENTIAN FAMILY |
| | | pl. 221 |

An uncharacteristically large GENTIAN, the stalk will rise 3- to 5-feet high. The blossoms are pale green and symmetrical (four-petals, four-sepals, four-stamens). The leaves are linear, situated in whorls with the flowers placed in the axils. Found on the fringes of meadows and named after the botanist John Fraser; *speciosa* means "showy." June to August.

| **DOGBANE, SPREADING** | *Apocynum* | DOGBANE FAMILY |
| | *androsaemifolium* | pl. 134 |

This is a small roadside shrub-like plant that will escape your attention unless you stop and take the time to investigate it. The flowers are small, pink or white bell-shaped blossoms on top of 12-inch stems. The leaves are drooping, oval-shaped and arranged oppositely. It prefers damp flats and hillsides from 2,000- to 8,000-feet. **Dogbane** comes from the Greek word *Apocynum*, meaning "noxious to dogs," referring to the poisonous "milk" the plant exudes. Indians used the fibers from the stems, which are very soft when dried, for weaving blankets and making ropes, nets and fishing line. June to September.

| **DOGWOOD, CREEK** | *Cornus stolonifera* | DOGWOOD FAMILY |
| | | pl. 54 |

This plant is a shrub, not a tree. It is a diminutive cousin of *C. nuttalli* and puts on an equally impressive display of vibrant red leaves in the fall. The many small, white, four-petaled flowers form large clusters at the tips of the branches. The overall size of the shrub will rarely be larger than 9- to 10-feet. It likes lakeshores and streambanks where there is an abundance of water. June to July.

| **DOGWOOD, PACIFIC** | *Cornus nuttallii* | DOGWOOD FAMILY |
| | | pl. 49 |

The **Dogwood** tree can be enjoyed in all seasons, but primarily it is Yosemite Valley's signal to begin spring. From this tree's bare branches unfurl creamy-white bracts (modified leaves) with a button-like central cluster of many tiny, green flowers. As the bracts mature and drop, the distinctively veined leaves begin to appear. Throughout the summer, the tree stands dwarfed and inconspicuous under the surrounding conifers, lazily blowing in the breezes. With the approach of fall, the green flowers have already formed clusters of red-orange fruits (drupes) balanced on the tips of their branches while the green leaves turn a flaming crimson. Once again the **Dogwood** emerges as the star of the forest.

| **DRABA, LEMMON'S** | *Draba lemmonii* | MUSTARD FAMILY |
| | | pl. 66 |

This is another one of those vibrant, spectacular alpine flowers, but to see it requires hiking into that wonderful "world above the trees." Look for it on the plateau of Mt. Dana and around Mt. Lyell. This tiny MUSTARD is a translucent yellow, four-petaled flower on the end of a hairy, 5- to 12-inch stem. The hairy leaves are spatula-like and clustered in a rosette close to the ground. It is named after John Lemmon, who first collected this plant on Mt. Lyell in 1878. It is one of the first alpine flowers to bloom. July to August.

ELDERBERRY, BLUE   *Sambucus caerulea*   HONEYSUCKLE FAMILY
pl. 60

This plant is really a shrub, growing large enough so as to appear to be a small tree. It has a lacy cluster of tiny white flowers, 2- to 6-inches, that last throughout the summer. As the season wanes they will turn to blue berries. The leaves are deep green and opposite, each stem having five to nine in the group. It is found from the foothills to 10,000-feet, along streams or moist slopes. April to August.

ELEPHANTS HEAD, BULL   *Pedicularis groenlandica*   FIGWORT FAMILY
pl. 171

Here's your chance to see pink elephants without ever touching a drop of your favorite elixir!! On close inspection each two-lipped flower forms a perfect pink elephant's head, with large floppy ears and an up-pointed trunk. Every tiny head is placed alternately around the terminal spike, with the "trunk" reaching outward as if searching for a handout. The leaves are lancelike and deeply cut, resembling a lacy fern frond, and are purple early in the season. The stems are 1- to 2-feet talland can be found in wet meadows from 6,000- to 12,000-feet. *Pedicularis* means "louse" (plural of lice — see **Elephants Head, Little**) and *groenlandica* means "of Greenland." June to August.

ELEPHANTS HEAD, LITTLE   *Pedicularis attolens*   FIGWORT FAMILY
pl. 172

Very similar to **Bull Elephants Head** except that it is smaller, the "trunk" is shorter and the "ears" are longer and hang lower. It will also have light pink or white markings on all five-petals. The blooms can be found in upper elevations to 12,000-feet. The members of the genus *Pedicularis* are *Lousewarts* (lice flowers). They are also partial root parasites (notice the purple leaves at the beginning of the season) which makes pasturage poor and causes livestock to be undernourished and susceptible to ecto-parasites (lice). *Pedicularis* means "louse" (lice) and *attolens* means "upraised." June to August.

FALSE SOLOMON'S SEAL   *Smilacina racemosa*   LILY FAMILY
pl. 31

The tiny white flowers of this lily are found at the tip of a single unbranched stem that rises 1- to 3-feet above the ground. The blossoms are star-shaped and appear to be branched along the length of the terminal spike. The parallel-veined leaves are 2- to 5-inches long clasping the stem. As the blossoms fade, they are replaced by red berries that are toxic. It can be found growing from 4,000- to 7,000-feet in shaded woods, especially the creek areas along Highway 41 between Wawona and Chinquapin. April to June.

FAREWELL-TO-SPRING   *Clarkia williamsonii*   EVENING PRIMROSE FAMILY
pl. 117

As its name suggests, this is the harbinger to the end of the flower season in its particular locale. It can be found from the foothills to 5,000-feet adding splashes of pink to the browning grasses surrounding it. The 1½-inch blossom has four wedge-shaped petals with a distinctive dark spot on the outside edge. The stems will always be just tall enough to reach above the competing grasses and the buds stand upright. It prefers dry open slopes and fields. The genus name *Clarkia,* honors William Clark of the Lewis and Clark expedition and the species name *williamsonii,* honors Lt. Robert Williamson, leader of a railway survey in the mid-eighteenth century. May to July.

FIDDLE NECK   *Amsinckia intermedia*   FORGET-ME-NOT FAMILY
pl. 112

This early bloomer in the foothills will attract attention, even from a rapidly moving vehicle. The flower head is a downward-coiled cluster of tiny (1/8-inch) yellow-orange flowers. The petals are joined to form a funnel-shaped blossom surrounded by dense, bristly hairs. The leaves are lancelike and finely toothed on stems 1- to 3-feet tall. The coiled flowering spike resembles the neck of a fiddle, hence the common name. April to May.

FIESTA FLOWER   *Pholistoma auritum*   WATERLEAF FAMILY
pl. 214

This vine-like plant most often is found intertwined around other flowering plants (especially **Redbuds**) creating a variety of spring colors and shapes. The **Fiesta Flower** has lavender-to-purple, bowl-like blossoms with five nipple-like projections. The 1- to 4-inch stems have reversed prickles. The leaf shape resembles the **Dandelion** leaf, pinnate, lancelike and lobes pointing downward. This foothill plant grows on shaded slopes below 4,500-feet. March to May.

FIREWEED

FIREWEED	*Epilobium angustifolium*	EVENING PRIMROSE FAMILY
		pl. 169

Once again nature has provided a beautiful solution to adversity. When man or fire destroys the ground cover of an area, it presents the opportunity for this flaming magenta flower to grow. It prefers moist areas, meadow fringes or along roadsides at most any elevation up to timberline. The long stalk, 2- to 6-feet tall, has alternate, lancelike leaves with the blossom forming a terminal spike. You will rarely see all of the four-petaled blossoms open at one time; the flowers on the bottom open first and progressively bloom up the stalk. Toward the end of the season, when the flowers have opened at the top, the bottom flowers have begun producing a distinctive four-sided seedpod. Later in the season the **Fireweed** will usually display seedpods, fresh buds, and open blossoms simultaneously! *Epilobium* means "above ovary" (referring to the fact that all *Epilobiums* have inferior ovaries and the ovary looks like the flower stem); *angustifolium* means "narrow-leaved." June to September.

FIREWEED, SMOOTHSTEM	*Epilobium glaberrimum*	EVENING PRIMROSE FAMILY
		pl. 124

This **Fireweed** bears little resemblance to its more showy cousin. It stands 1- to 3-feet tall with lancelike, opposite leaves. The small (1- to 1½-inch wide) blossoms are four-petaled, bi-lobed, and are located near the top of the stem. It enjoys wet places and can be found in abundance around Misquito Creek on Highway 41. June to August.

FLAX, BLUE	*Linum perenne*	FLAX FAMILY
	ssp. *lewissi*	**pl. 189**

The **Flax** is a bright blue, five-petaled flower, ¾- to 1½-inches wide, growing on top of delicate stems up to 30-inches high. The short leaves are linear and alternate. It is found in the Park's coniferous forests and exposed ridges. June to September.

FOXGLOVE	*Digitalis purpurea*	FIGWORT FAMILY
		pl. 167

This uncommon plant is spectacular when encountered. It is an alien, but not unwanted because of the marvelous beauty it adds to a shady area or glen. The blossoms are at the top of a 2- to 7-foot stalk cascading downward on only one side. Each white, pink, or lavender two-lipped tubular blossom has maroon speckles in the throat. The long leaves are oval shaped and scalloped. Digitalis, the heart medicine, is derived from this species, but is highly toxic if not correctly administered. The plants are commonly found along the South Fork of the Merced River, where Highway 41 crosses at Wawona, and behind the Valley Visitor Center. June to July.

FRITILLARY, DAVIDSON'S	*Fritillaria pinetorum*	LILY FAMILY
		pl. 220

The **Fritillaries** are a delightfully delicate member of the LILY clan and this one is no exception! It grows in the woods along the trail to Sentinel Dome near the creek crossing. The blossoms are six-petaled and brown with green and yellow mottling. They stand erect at the end of 6- to 16-inch stems. Leaves are grass-like and whorled around the thin stem. They are not common, so the thrill of discovering one can highlight any summer afternoon. June to July.

FUCHSIA, CALIFORNIA	*Zauschneria californica*	EVENING PRIMROSE FAMILY
		pl. 142

These shrub-shaped, leafy plants flower late in the summer when most others have gone to seed. The brilliant red (1½-inch) tubular flowers have petals folded back to reveal protruding anthers. The leaves are ½- to 1½-inches long, broad, green and lancelike. It loves dry slopes and ridges and produces a vibrant display of color against the barest of granite. It grows from sea level to above 7,000-feet, changing only slightly with elevation. Sometimes called **"Hummingbird Trumpet"** because Hummingbirds are attracted to the red blossoms and are the plant's pollinators. Indians used the leaves to make a tea to relieve kidney and bladder infections. August to October.

| GAYOPHYTUM | *Gayophytum heterozygum* | EVENING PRIMROSE FAMILY **pl. 14** |

There are six different species of *Gayophytum* in Yosemite and all are so similar that only the finest detail in the seedpod identifies them. It is therefore understandable why the Latin names — *Gay*, after the botanist Claude Gay, *phytum*, "plant" and *heterozygum*, "different (genetic) link," were given. The flowers are tiny (¼-inch wide), obscure, four-petaled and sparsely scattered on the 24-inch multibranched stem. It grows from 4,000- to 10,000-feet on dry, open flats or slopes. July to August.

| GENTIAN, ALPINE | *Gentiana newberryi* | GENTIAN FAMILY **pl. 15** |

This GENTIAN is abundant in Tuolumne Meadows growing alongside the **Hikers Gentian** (*G. simplex*) at elevations between 7,000- to 12,000-feet. This is a short, white version of GENTIANS found at lower elevations. Since the leaves are usually hidden in meadow grass, it appears that the four-petaled, funnel-shaped blossoms exist by themselves. The throat is often dotted in green; the calyx is ribbed. Its leaves are broad and basal on short (3- to 6-inch) stems. July to August.

| GENTIAN, HIKERS | *Gentiana simplex* | GENTIAN FAMILY **pl. 188** |

GENTIANS are a colorful component of late season high mountain meadows. The blossom is four-petaled and funnel-shaped, with the petals flaring outward toward the axil. The lobes of the calyx (plural of sepal) are plain, not dark-ribbed. The 6- to 16-inch stem has only one blossom at its terminus, although each plant may have several stems. It has three to six pairs of lancelike leaves arranged oppositely. *Gentiana* was named after Gentius, the King of Illyria, who found the herb to have a healing effect on his malaria-stricken troops. June to August.

| GERANIUM, WILD | *Geranium richardsonii* | GERANIUM FAMILY **pl. 122** |

This is a wild cousin to our common yard **Geranium**. It has the same identifying characteristic, a crane-like beak at the end of the pistil, hence its other name "Cranesbill." Its petals are rounded, pale pink with purple veins at the end of 12- to 24-inch branched stems. The leaves are deeply cut and palm-shaped. It favors moist mountain meadows. *Geranium* means "crane;" *richardsonii* after Sir John Richardson, an eighteenth century naturalist. July to August.

| GILIA, BRIDGE'S | *Gilia leptalea* | PHLOX FAMILY **pl. 205** |

This **Gilia** creates massive carpets of purple color in forest openings. The blossom is tubular and five-petaled. Leaves are narrow and lancelike, but generally are not noticed unless you part the blossoms and look close to the ground. This purple show can be seen in the sandy, open areas around Gin Flat. June to July.

| GILIA, SCARLET | *Ipomopsis aggregata* | PHLOX FAMILY **pl. 152** |

Scarlet Gilias are known to light up entire hillsides with bright red color. The blossom is a 1-inch tube that abruptly flares into a perfect five-point star with only its stamens protruding. The star face is marked by a mottling of yellow. The stems are 1- to 2-feet tall; the leaves are narrow and pinnately-dissected. The Hummingbird is its pollinator, attracted by the brilliant red color of the blossom. It prefers dry, sunny, well-drained hillsides. *Ipomopsis* means "of striking appearance" and *aggregata* means "flocking together." June to August.

| GINGER, WILD | *Asarum hartwegii* | BIRTHWORT FAMILY **pl. 219** |

Early settlers, hungry for the exotic ginger, mistook this plant for the real thing, but the only similarity between the two is the fragrance. This herb is most frequently recognized by its large, shiny, heart-shaped leaves. Only after close examination, moving the leaves aside, do the brown petals become apparent. Each petal is triangular, with the base extending from a bowl to become pointed and curling at the tip. It can be found growing along moist streambanks and in dense, wet woods, especially around Mirror Lake, and Mosquito Creek on Highway 41. May to June.

GOLDENROD, ALPINE   *Solidago multiradiata*   SUNFLOWER FAMILY
pl. 93

This shorter (12-inch) version of the **Meadow Goldenrod** grows above 8,000 feet and has yellow ray flowers (approximately 13 per head). The leaves are hairy, spatula-shaped and wavy. They are found along the roadside in Tuolumne Meadows and subalpine rock fields. June to September.

GOLDENROD, MEADOW   *Solidago canadensis*   SUNFLOWER FAMILY
pl. 94

Another signal of the end of summer is the appearance of the vibrant yellow **Goldenrod**. Each flower consists of many florets, both ray flowers and disk flowers, and the spike is composed of many flower heads, giving it the appearance of a 3- to 7-inch bottle brush. The leaves are many, lancelike, and sharply toothed. It is found throughout Yosemite in meadows and along moist roadsides, 3,000- to 8,000-feet. It was used by early miners as a divining rod to find water and gold, but the Indians had a more practical use, they ground it and made a poultice for sores and toothaches. *Solidago* means "healer" and *canadensis* means "from Canada." July to September.

GOLDENROD, NARROW   *Solidago occidentalis*   SUNFLOWER FAMILY
pl. 90

This tall Goldenrod (up to 32-inches) has several stems per cluster. The small yellow flower heads are in a flat grouping, consisting of 16 to 20 ray flowers and 8 to 14 disk flowers. The smooth stem has lancelike leaves about 6-inches long. It grows in moist areas up to 8,000-feet. July to September.

GRASS NUTS   *Brodiaea laxa*   AMARYLLIS FAMILY
pl. 201

This plant is very similar to the **Harvest Brodiaea** except the color is a lighter sky blue and the stem branches into many stemlets, each containing a larger (1-inch) funnel-shaped blossom. Found around El Portal and surrounding foothills. April to July.

GRASS-OF-PARNASSUS   *Parnassia palustris*   SAXIFRAGE FAMILY
var. *californica*   pl. 13

This late bloomer frequents marshy areas alongside **Elephants Heads, Monkshoods** and **Bistorts**. The blossoms have five petals that are creamy-white to yellow with greenish veins. The stems are 6- to 18-inches high and rise out of basal, elliptic leaves. July to October.

GROUNDSEL,   *Senecio triangularis*   SUNFLOWER FAMILY
ARROWLEAF   pl. 108

Not to be confused with the similar **Single-stemmed Groundsel**. This species grows alongside streambanks or seeps. Its leaves are distinctly arrow-shaped, long and triangular. The tall stems average 36-inches including the yellow flowers that sit on top. In the Tuolumne area, it grows in wilderness gardens consisting of **Stickseed, Delphinium, Crimson Columbine, Lupine,** and **Swamp Onion.** A portion of the trail to Mt. Dana passes through one such spectacular garden. June to September.

GROUNDSEL,   *Senecio integerrimus*   SUNFLOWER FAMILY
SINGLE-STEMMED   pl. 104

You can see this distinguished flower all the way from the foothills to timberline, mingling among the conifers. The compound flower sits upon a tall, 6- to 36-inch, single stem. The blossom is a congested arrangement of tiny yellow flowers. The leaves are spoon-like and grouped at the base. It prefers dry, well-drained forest floors. *Senacio* means "old man" because the plant has the appearance of a bald old man after the seeds have blown away, and *integerrimus* means "undivided (leaves)." May to July.

HEATHER, MOUNTAIN   *Phyllodoce breweri*   HEATH FAMILY
pl. 153

This plant adds a rich green appearance to the subalpine forests and the rocky outcroppings above timberline. For a short time, immediately after the snow melts, it will have ½-inch pink-to-red bell-shaped blossoms clustered at the end of 6- to 12-inch stems. The stamens protrude above the back-curled petals. The leaves look like fir needles clustered along the woody stem. *Phyllodoce* means "sea nymph" and *breweri* is named after William Brewer, California's first state botanist. June to July.

HEATHER, WHITE *Cassiope mertensiana* HEATH FAMILY
pl. 23

When you encounter this **Heather** for the first time it is easy to understand why John Muir delighted in its presence. The blossoms are nodding white bells with red sepals attached to the base. It is a short 4- to 12-inch, shrub that clings to moist rocky outcroppings at or above timberline. The leaves are fir-like needles tightly gripping the stems. One place to find this hardy plant is above Vogelsang High Sierra Camp. Again, Greek mythology plays a part in the botanical naming of a plant: *Cassiope* was Queen Cassiope of Ethiopia and *mertensiana* is named after a German botanist, Franz Mertens. July to August.

HEDGE NETTLE, *Stachys albens* MINT FAMILY
WHITESTEM pl. 32

The prominent feature of this plant is the covering of fine, cobwebby hairs along the terminal spike, especially as the season advances. The blossoms are whorled about the stem in clusters, getting tighter toward the tip. They are two-lipped, the upper erect, the lower spreading. The stem is typical of a MINT, four-sided or "square." It stands 1- to 4-feet high, with the leaves triangular and opposite. It is found in marshy areas and wet meadows below 8,000-feet. The genus *Stachys* does not have stinging hairs as the **Stinging Nettle** in the NETTLE FAMILY *(Urticaceae)*. The name "nettle" which we associate with "stinging" is also used in the MINT and POTATO families which do not have stinging hairs (so much for common names). June to October.

HORKELIA, DUSKY *Horkelia fusca* ROSE FAMILY
pl. 11

This plant is a perennial herb with long feather-like leaves, mostly basal, with a stem 6- to 18-inches tall rising from the center. The flower has five wedge-shaped petals that grow from a bowl-like base. It can be found in open woodlands and meadow edges. May to July.

HYSSOP, GIANT *Agastache urticifolia* MINT FAMILY
pl. 173

The flowers form a terminal spike featuring clusters of tubular, two-lipped blossoms with two pairs of protruding stamens. The color will vary from white or rose to purple. The leaves are triangular, opposite, and toothed on a "square" (typical of the MINT) stalk up to 5-feet tall. It is found along meadow fringes, streambanks and roadways from 3,000- to 7,000-feet. Be sure to take a long admiring look when first observed, for the blossoms will only last a couple of days. *Agastache* means "many spikes" and *urticifolia* means "nettle-like leaves." June to September.

INDIAN HEMP *Apocynum cannabinum* DOGBANE FAMILY
pl. 52

This plant is most noticeable in the fall when it turns a blazing yellow. Its abundant, broad, lancelike leaves, provide a spectacular fall show. It likes streambanks and moist meadow fringes and is prevalent throughout Yosemite Valley along the Merced River. The north side of Leidig Meadow provides an especially nice grouping. It can grow as high as 5-feet. In the early summer it will have white-to-pink bell-shaped flowers scattered along the stem. The Yosemite Indians used the tough fiber from the stems to make blankets, twine, rope, fishing line and to weave their baskets. Although the leaves are poisonous to cattle and horses, the roots were used as a heart stimulant and as a laxative. *Apocynum* means "Dogbane" and *cannabinum* means "hemplike." June to July.

INDIAN PINK *Silene californica* PINK FAMILY
pl. 126

The **Indian Pink** is an uncommon but brightly colored member of the foothill community. Its crimson flower has five-petals, each one deeply cut into four-additional lobes, giving it the appearance of having been hand-trimmed with *pinking sheers*. Its stems and leaves secrete a sticky substance that can snare small insects, hence the nickname **"Catchfly."** The leaves are oval shaped and opposite. Pinks are always found in shady areas. March to July.

IRIS, WILD   *Iris missouriensis*   IRIS FAMILY
                                                        pl. 216

This lovely wildflower is also know as **Western Blue Flag.** Its graceful, delicate blossom suggests three ballerinas (the petals) standing together upright (the two on either side look like they are doing a backbend). The petals are predominantly blue with some yellow-orange and white markings toward the center. These "ballerinas" dance atop a stout 8- to 20-inch stalk rising out of a clump of tough, sword-shaped leaves. The leaves and seedpod remain blue-gray-green long after the early blossom has faded. Found in moist meadows 4,000- to 8,500-feet. *Iris* comes from Iris, Greek Goddess of the Rainbow and *missouriensis* means "Missouri." The edges of the sword-shaped leaves were used by some Indians to make twine to capture small animals. The presence of this flower is an indication of over-grazing. Sheep and cattle seem aware of its toxicity and won't eat it, eventually it fills the meadow. East side of El Capitan Meadow is a prime example of this. May to July.

JIMSON WEED   *Datura meteloides*   NIGHTSHADE FAMILY
                                                        pl. 4

This large, impressive trumpet-shaped flower blooms late in the season and can be found near Cascade Creek along Highway 140. The blossom is large (4- to 8-inches long) with a tubular calyx wrapped around the base. The wavy leaves are grayish and oval. It acts like a creeper, staying close to the ground. It is thought to have been introduced from Mexico. Some Indian tribes used an extract from this plant in some of their religious ceremonies. "Caution" all parts of this plant are "extremely poisonous" and can cause "death." June to October.

KLAMATH WEED   *Hypericum perforatum*   ST. JOHN'S WORT FAMILY
                                                        pl. 69

This flower is similar to **St. John's Wort,** *(H. formosum)* except that it is multibranched growing from 4- to 16-inches tall and appears to be more like a shrub. The leaves are lancelike and folded upward. It is an aggressive weed in Yosemite Valley, so the Klamath Moth was introduced because it proved to be a biological control. June to September.

LADIES TRESSES,   *Spiranthes*   ORCHID FAMILY
HOODED   *romanzoffiana*   **pl. 39**

Tiny **Orchid** flowers are arranged on a greenish-white spike, like a spiral staircase, on the upper half of the 4- to 18-inch stem. The top two petals form a hood over the rest of the flower. The leaves are lancelike and basal. It frequents moist high meadows from 5,000- to 10,000-feet. June to August.

LABRADOR TEA   *Ledum glandulosum*   HEATH FAMILY
                            var. *californicum*   **pl. 50**

This lovely shrub can be seen along subalpine creeks and lakesides. The white, 3- to 4-inch wide flowers cluster at the end of stalks 2- to 5-feet high. They are five-petaled and have five to twelve stamens standing upright. The leaves are dark-green and very tough, with glands on the underside. The name "tea" is deceiving for it is poisonous. June to August.

LARKSPUR   *Delphinium nuttallianum*   BUTTERCUP FAMILY
                                                        pl. 197

This plant strongly resembles the **Tower Larkspur** in color and blossom shape, except that it is shorter (8- to 18-inches) and the two lower petals are deeply bi-lobed. The leaf shape is more rounded, but still intricately divided into sharp tips. It grows on meadow fringes and trailsides in middle elevations. *Delphinium* means "Dolphin," for the buds are shaped in the image of a Dolphin, and **"Larkspur"** is from the sepal having a spur resembling the spur on the back toe of a Lark. April to July.

LARKSPUR, TOWER   *Delphinium glaucum*   BUTTERCUP FAMILY
     pl. 198

    Larkspurs are distinctive members of both wetland and dry communities. The **Tower** species is the tallest (3- to 6-feet) and easiest to identify. The blossom consists of five sharp-pointed purple sepals joined at the back to form a spur, making this a favorite for hummingbirds. The two lower petals are not bi-lobed. The leaves are dull green and have sharp, deep palm-like lobes. Its habitat is high mountain marshy gardens. This flower was called **"Sleep-Root"** by some Indians, and it is thought they used the juice to dull the senses of an opponent during games and gambling. July to September.

LAUREL, ALPINE   *Kalmia polifolia*   HEATH FAMILY
     var. *microphylla*   **pl. 154**

    This tiny jewel of the high country stands out because of its flowers as well as its striking evergreen leaves. When in bloom the flowers are the stars, for they resemble shallow, rose-colored cups ½-inch wide. The ten tiny stamens are tucked away in "spring-loaded" pouches on the petals. When a pollinator jostles the plant they explode, casting their pollen onto the insect. The leaves are paired, lancelike and curled back along the side margins, giving them an even narrower appearance. It has 3- to 8-inch stems and grows in the subalpine and alpine meadows. *Kalmia* is named after the Swedish botanist Peter Kalm; *poli* means "gray" and *folia* means "leaf." The plant is poisonous and used to be called Sheepkill or Lambkill because of this. June to August.

LESSINGIA, SIERRA   *Lessingia leptoclada*   SUNFLOWER FAMILY
     pl. 202

    Sometimes called the harbinger of fall, this small lavender blossom branches and rebranches throughout late summer until roadsides appear to be a sea of color. The inner blossom consists of all disk (tubular) flowers, but the outer flowers are enlarged and look like ray flowers. The mature branches grow up to 24-inches tall. Leaves are woolly and sparse. **Lessingia** grows on dry flats and along roadsides, and was a favorite late summer flower of Mary Curry Tresidder. She fondly referred to it as **"Summer Lavender."** *Lessingia* is named after the German botanist, Christian Lessing; *leptoclada* means "with thin twigs." July to September.

LILY, CAMAS   *Camassia leichtlinii*   LILY FAMILY
     ssp. *suksdorfii*   **pl. 187**

    This plant is considered one of the most beautiful flowers to be found in wet mountain meadows. **Bistorts** (white), **Shooting Stars** (pink, yellow and maroon), and this lovely flower (blue) create a vibrant floral display during spring. It is a symmetrical, six-petaled, royal blue blossom, accented by six bright gold anthers. There are 4 to 12 blossoms on a single erect stem, 12- to 36-inches tall, rising out of a whorl of basal leaves. The buds open late in the day and will usually wither within 24 hours, so afternoon is the best time to see them. All of the western Indians depended on Camas bulbs as a staple in their diet. Destruction of the Camas fields by settlers' hogs fueled a bloody war with the Nez Perce Nation in Washington State. *Camas,* meaning "sweet" comes from the Chinook language. Crane Flat is an excellent place to see the **Camas Lily.** May to June.

LILY, CORN   *Veratrum californicum*   LILY FAMILY
     pl. 37

    In the early spring, **Corn Lilies** appear in great clusters, their poisonous leaves tightly wrapped around a thick immature stalk. Soon the broad, ribbed leaves unfurl and a meadow is transformed into a "mountain corn field." As the plants reach their full height, 3- to 6-feet, flowers form at the top of the centered stalk. The tassels consist of six-petaled flowers, each petal having a green v-shaped spot at the base. Conditions must be just right for this plant to bloom; some years the **Corn Lily** is barren of blossoms. It grows from 6,000- to 10,000-feet. June to July.

LILY, GLOBE   *Calochortus albus*   LILY FAMILY
     pl. 24

    Also known as **"Fairy Lantern"** this is an exquisite flower that grows at low elevations and blooms early in the season. Its blossoms remind you of oriental lanterns dangling in the gentle spring breezes. The globes are actually three 1-inch petals that are joined at the tips to form a nodding orb. The leaves are lancelike appearing as long, broad blades of grass. They flatter rocky hillsides and roadcuts below 3,000-feet. *Calochortus* comes from the Greek words *kalos* meaning "beautiful" and *chortus;* "grass." April to June.

LILY, INDIAN POND *Nuphar polysepalum* WATER LILY FAMILY
pl. 110

This aquatic plant can be found in several locations in the Park. One such pond, in Cook's Meadow, can be depended upon to produce large quantities of this bright yellow flower. Its tight, chalice-shaped, yellow blossom never seems to fully open. The leaves are large (4- to 18-inches), heart shaped, and float lazily on the water's surface. April to July.

LILY, KELLY'S TIGER *Lilium kelleyanum* LILY FAMILY
pl. 114

This long and lanky looking **Lily** is not common in Yosemite and requires a diligent search through moist bogs. The blossom hangs downward from a 2- to 6-foot stout stem. Its six orange petals recurve backward fully and allow the anthers and styles (the reproductive organs) to protrude. The leaves are whorled and oblong. July to August.

LILY, MARIPOSA *Calochortus leichtlinii* LILY FAMILY
pl. 9

Most people consider the butterfly a most beautiful creature to behold. This flower must have suggested that beauty to an early botanist, for mariposa means "butterfly" in Spanish. The three-petaled, three-sepaled blossom is predominantly white, with a dark red-purple spot (gray at higher elevations) at the base. The flower waves above an 8- to 16-inch stem, with sparse linear leaves. It is found in dry forests and hillsides at all elevations in the Park. *Calochortus* means "beautiful grass" and *leichtlinii* is named after the German horticulturist, Max Leichtlin. June to August.

LILY, SMALL LEOPARD *Lilium parvum* LILY FAMILY
pl. 115

A smaller, common cousin to **Kelly's Tiger Lily** *(L. kelleyanum).* Its bell-shaped, six-petaled flowers stand erect, flaring outward (instead of drooping down) and the throat is marked with distinctive maroon spots. The leaves are lancelike, scattered along a 2- to 4-foot stem. It is neighbors with the **Lungwort** and **Groundsel** along streambanks and moist bogs, primarily from 6,000- to 9,000-feet. June to July.

LILY, WASHINGTON *Lilium washingtonianum* LILY FAMILY
pl. 26

An uncommon but spectacular wildflower to find is this *Easter-Lily*-like plant. The snow-white flower tube extends two-thirds of the petal length before curling back. Some purple dots can be seen on the throat area. The flowers are large (3- to 5-inches) and are on the branching end of its 3- to 8-foot stems. The leaves are large whorled groupings and are quite symmetrical. They grow along Highway 41 on either side of Chinquapin and on the Tioga Road (120 East) just east of the South Fork of the Tuolumne River. Individual blossoms last only a short time, but the flowers can often be seen through July. The name has a bit of history. The early settlers named it the "Lady Washington Lily" after Martha Washington, our first "first lady," and botanist Dr. Albert Kellogg decided to break all rules of flower identification when he gave this plant the settlers' common name. July to August.

LIVE-FOREVER *Dudleya cymosa* SEDUM FAMILY
pl. 147

This is a succulent found enhancing dry rocky cracks and ledges early in the year. The leaves are thick, fleshy rosettes with pointed ends. The flowers are yellow, with red at the tips, balancing on the top of 4- to 6-inch stems. It is found at lower elevations. April to June.

LOCOWEED *Astragalus bolanderi* PEA FAMILY
pl. 103

Locoweed was named because when soil contains the chemical selenium, it causes horses who feel compelled to eat it to "go crazy." It is a visually attractive plant to humans. The creamy-white to yellow pea-shaped blossoms are randomly arranged at the stem ends. The 3- to 6-inch leaves are symmetrical and made up of 17 to 27 leaflets. It stands 12- to 20-inches tall and likes open forests or gravelly hillsides from 5,000- to 10,000-feet. In the fall it produces the typical peapods. With the late summer breezes, the pods dry and produce a rattling noise, because of this sound it is also called **"Rattleweed."** *Astragalus* means "crazy" and *bolanderi* is named after Henry Bolander, a diligent collector of Yosemite plants and California's State Botanist in 1864. It is very common in Peregoy Meadow and White Wolf Meadow from July to August.

LOMATIUM, FERN-LEAVED   *Lomatium dissectum*   CARROT FAMILY
pl. 107

This plant has the distinctive foliage of the CARROT FAMILY. The leaves are deeply cut several times making them appear like fine lace. The flowers consist of many blossoms in an umbrella shape, mostly yellow but sometimes purple. It grows 3- to 5-feet tall in rocky places and along roadsides. Look for it around Hetch Hetchy. April to June.

LOTUS, NARROWLEAF   *Lotus oblongifolius*   PEA FAMILY
pl. 102

Lotus, Lotus everywhere! Wander through the western half of El Capitan Meadow in early summer and you will not be able to overlook this bushy, bi-colored (yellow and white) pea-shaped flower. Each flower has a yellow banner petal with white lower petals. The blossoms often appear in groups of three. The bright green leaves are actually made up of 7 to 11 leaflets per branch, each stem is multibranched, giving it the tangled appearance of a shrub (although it is not). This **Lotus** has a unique provision to guarantee successful pollination. When a bee lands on a wing petal the keel is forced open, exposing the stigma and spraying pollen on the intruder. May to August.

LOTUS, SILVERLEAF   *Lotus argophyllus*   PEA FAMILY
pl. 98

Although not as conspicuous as other **Lotus** plants, this **Lotus** is just as pretty as the others. It is a creeper that sends out long runners, with pea-shaped yellow flowers located at the axil of the leaves and stem. The leaflets are oval and clustered in groupings of three to five, with both the leaves and stems hairy. It forms large mats on dry, well-drained areas below 6,000-feet. Look for it along the Wawona Road near Chinquapin. May to July.

LOUSEWORT, DWARF   *Pedicularis semibarbata*   FIGWORT FAMILY
pl. 101

This distinctly different little plant will be found clinging to the ground on moderate to upper elevation forest floors. Its leaves are more prominent than its blossoms, which are yellow tubular flowers with red tints. A beaked upper lip protrudes and curls downward. The 2- to 6-inch leaves resemble deeply cut Fern fronds. **Lousewort** means "lice flower" (see **Little Elephants Head**). May to July.

LUNGWORT, MOUNTAIN   *Mertensia ciliata*   FORGET-ME-NOT FAMILY
var. *stomatechoides*   pl. 215

This is a tall (up to 5-feet) plant with nodding, delicate blue, ½-inch tubular blossoms that undulate in gentle summer breezes. The stems are erect; with the leaves lancelike and alternate. It can be found on the edges of moist mountain meadows and streambanks mingling with **Groundsel** and **Small Leopard Lilies.** It is often referred to as **"Mountain Bluebell."** Herbalists of the 16th and 17th centuries believed it could be used to cure lung ailments, hence its name **"Lungwort"** (wort means "flower"). *Mertensia* is named after the German botanist, Franz Mertens, and *ciliata* means "with hairy edges." 4,000-to 6,000-feet. June to August.

LUPINE, BREWER'S   *Lupinus breweri*   PEA FAMILY
pl. 194

There are over 80 species of **Lupine** in California; this is a low, matting variety, rarely taller than 6-inches. It can be found covering the roadsides of the Tioga and Glacier Point Roads. The flowers are pea-shaped and small, with a white spot in the center of the banner petal. The palm-like leaves are silvery with short hairs. *Lupinus* means "wolf" (see **Bush Lupine**). June to August.

LUPINE, BROADLEAF   *Lupinus latifolius*   PEA FAMILY
pl. 193

Lupines comprise one of the largest and most confusing genera in California. The flower is the most identifying characteristic and will hold true throughout the genus. Identifying an individual species can often be time-consuming and frustrating, so in most cases one is satisfied with calling it **"Lupine."** All **Lupine** are pea-shaped. The blossom is five-petaled and two-lipped, with the upper petal (banner), the lower petal (keel), and side petals (wings) making up the whole. The leaves of this species have seven to nine wide, rounded lobes, palmately arranged. The Broadleaf species is a tall, bushy plant that likes moist meadow fringes and roadsides. It grows at most elevations up to timberline. *Lupinus* means "wolf" and *latifolius* means "broad-leaf" (see **Bush Lupine** for further information on origin of "wolf"). April to August.

LUPINE, BUSH   *Lupinus albifrons*   PEA FAMILY
pl. 190

This **Lupine** is very similar to **Broadleaf Lupine** *(L. latifolius)* except that it grows at lower elevations (El Portal to Yosemite Valley) on dry, rocky roads and hillsides. The plant grows to 5-feet and has long spikes of deep blue blossoms. The leaves are palm-like and profoundly cut with sharp tips. Old world beliefs led people to think this plant robbed the soil of nourishment so they named it **Lupine,** meaning "wolf." Since then we have learned the opposite is true: members of this family provide a source of nitrogen to the soil, but still the name persists. April to June.

LUPINE, HARLEQUIN   *Lupinus stiversii*   PEA FAMILY
pl. 196

If you were to pick a favorite out of the 23 species of Yosemite **Lupines,** it would have to be the **Harlequin!** It combines the individual characteristics of each species into one spectacular, tri-colored blossom. The outer "wing" petals are pink, the "banner" petal yellow, and the "keel" petal white. Numerous blossoms are clustered (½- to 1½-inches) to form a terminal spike exploding with color. The leaves are palm-shaped with six to nine leaflets on 4- to 18-inch stems. It can be found in well-drained, sandy soil of Oak and Ponderosa Pine forests. April to July.

LUPINE, MINIATURE   *Lupinus bicolor*   PEA FAMILY
ssp. *microphyllus*   pl. 195

A short, ground-hugging version of its larger cousins. The flowers of this **Lupine** are tiny, blue and white, and whorled on a stem usually 8- to 18-inches above the ground. Its five to seven leaflets are linear and, of course, arranged in the typical palm-shape. It can be found covering the ground in large groupings along Highway 41 in the Wawona area. April to July.

LUPINE, WHITEWHORL   *Lupinus densiflorus*   PEA FAMILY
pl. 7

Here is proof that all **Lupines** are not blue! The white (sometimes pink) pea-shaped flowers are whorled around the stem forming a long terminal spike. The leaves are palm-shaped and feature seven to nine lobes. It is 1- to 3-feet tall and found on grassy hillsides at lower elevations. *Lupinus* means "wolf" (see **Bush Lupine**) and *densiflorus* means "dense flowers." April to June.

MADIA, COMMON   *Madia elegans*   SUNFLOWER FAMILY
pl. 82

This is a Sunflower-like flower occurring in dry, open forest areas, especially the west end of El Capitan Meadow. The base of each ray flower has a maroon or brown oval spot. A sub species of this plant is all yellow. The flowers open in late afternoon and close in the morning. The stems are well branched, up to 36-inches high; the leaves are linear and alternate. Both stem and leaves are quite sticky, giving it the nickname **"Tarweed."** It grows at elevations of 3,000- to 8,000-feet. June to August.

MANZANITA   *Arctostaphylos patula*   HEATH FAMILY
pl. 179

Many species of **Manzanita** grow throughout Yosemite and California, all easily recognized by even the neophyte. Some species create a mat close to the ground, and some grow to be 20-feet tall. Sometimes the miniscule distinctions between the species present frustrations. If **"Manzanita"** is not sufficient identification, we encourage you to refer to a traditional botanical reference volume for details for "keying out" the species. In general, the blossoms are pink or white, bell- or urn-shaped, from oval to round and the branches are usually crooked, hard, and covered by red, peeling bark. The blossoms turn into "berries" that resemble little apples which the Indians became adept at making into a cider. **Manzanita** means "little apple." Found from the foothills to 10,000-feet preferring sunny, dry slopes. Blooms April to June and berries June to August.

MARIGOLD, MARSH   *Caltha howellii*   BUTTERCUP FAMILY
                                                         pl. 6

This flower signals the beginning of spring in the high marshes. As the snow melts to a few sheltered patches, this perennial will send up stems 6- to 12-inches tall and bloom forth with a white, six-to-ten-sepaled blossom with yellow stamens. The leaves are bright and kidney-shaped. **Marsh Marigolds** tend to dominate the marshes as the season progresses. June to August.

MEADOW RUE   *Thalictrum fendleri*   BUTTERCUP FAMILY
                                                        pl. 218

On close inspection, this leafy, bushy plant produces small delicate flowers. The male, pollen-producing blossom, has long stamens hanging from the four to seven sepals. The female, seed-producing part, is found on a separate plant. There are no petals on either the male or the female flower. The leaves are deeply lobed and compound. It grows at elevations of 4,000- to 10,000-feet on moist streambanks. May to July.

MICROSERIS, NODDING   *Microseris nutans*   SUNFLOWER FAMILY
                                                              pl. 80

This **Dandelion**-like wildflower grows on the fringes of forests and meadows at middle elevations. The blossom has many narrow ray flowers, no disk flowers, and the buds droop downward prior to opening. The leaves are strap-like, with two to four pairs of sharp teeth arranged near the center of the blade along the 12-inch stem. May to August.

MILKWEED, PURPLE   *Asclepias cordifolia*   MILKWEED FAMILY
                                                              pl. 137

This MILKWEED is not nearly as common as its cousin, **Showy Milkweed,** but is just as spectacular and more colorful. Both the stems and the blossoms are reddish-purple. The blossoms are arranged in a sparse, umbrella shape, with the petals bent back as if facing a stiff breeze. The leaves are broad, clasping the stem, making each appear to be a "heart shape" *(cordifolia)*. *Asclepias* is named after the Greek founder of medicine, Aesculapias. The stems and leaves exude a bitter, milky substance which plays an important part in the life of the Monarch Butterfly (see **Showy Milkweed**). It prefers dry shaded forest areas below 5,000-feet. May to July.

MILKWEED, SHOWY   *Asclepias speciosa*   MILKWEED FAMILY
                                                           pl. 138

Of all the beautiful wildflowers in Yosemite, **Showy Milkweed** puts on the longest and most varied show! From early May, when it first sprouts a silvery gray stalk, until October, when the parachute-shaped seeds are carried in the breeze, their display is astounding! In June, after the plant has grown a 2- to 4-foot stalk, the delicate silvery, round buds begin to open. These buds form a sphere of many pointed, small, pink flowers. The leaves are oval or oblong, arranged oppositely, gradually turning gray-green as summer progresses. As the flowers wane, a burred seedpod forms. It makes a complete loop on the stem by folding back on itself, and then stands erect. September and October turn the leaves yellow and, finally, the woolly pods split open dramatically, releasing the feather-like seeds to be carried in the cool, gentle fall breezes to a new location. Each phase of its life is a beautiful sight to behold, and to witness the entire cycle is a grand experience. Another admirer of the **Showy Milkweed** is the Monarch Butterfly. In late spring and early summer, the Monarch caterpillar will gorge itself on the **Milkweed** leaves and absorb large quantities of its bitter-tasting poison "milk"-sap, making itself unappealing to would-be predators. *Asclepias* is named for Aesculapias, the Greek founder of medicine, and *speciosa* means "showy." The Indians used the stems as fiber for weaving and making ropes. Flowers May to August.

MINT, COYOTE　　　　*Monardella villosa*　　　MINT FAMILY
　　　　　　　　　　　　　　　　　　　　　　　　　pl. 206

　　The flowers on this MINT appear in spectacular blue to purple, whorled around the outside of a single head. The center is bare, resembling a green, balding scalp. The leaves are lancelike and opposite, exuding the typical pungent mint odor. It likes dry, sandy soil below 6,000-feet. A good place to see this MINT is on the north fringe of the Ahwahnee Meadow. June to July.

MINT, FIELD　　　　　*Mentha arvensis*　　　MINT FAMILY
　　　　　　　　　　　　　　　　　　　　　　　　pl. 175

　　A common plant in moist meadows, found throughout the summer. The blossoms are thick and compactly whorled around the "square" stem, typical of MINTS, with lancelike and opposite placed leaves directly below each flower. The leaves are sharply toothed and symmetrically placed on a 6- to 24-inch stem. June to September.

MOCK ORANGE　　　　*Philadelphus lewisii*　　SAXIFRAGE FAMILY
　　　　　　　　　　　　　　　　　　　　　　　　pl. 53

　　Mock Orange is probably the most noticeable of all the fragrances filling the air early in the spring season. It is classified as a shrub, and bears a waxy white blossom which reminds you of a stroll through a Southern California orange orchard. It prefers the rocky slopes of Yosemite Valley and the banks along the Merced River canyon near El Portal. May to July.

MONKEY FLOWER,　　　*Mimulus tilingii*　　　FIGWORT FAMILY
ALPINE　　　　　　　　　　　　　　　　　　pl. 97

　　This flower is similar to the **Common Monkey Flower,** except that the petioles are considerably longer than the petals and the stem has only one to three blossoms at its terminus. Usually found in wet places from 8,000- to 11,000-feet. *Mimulus* means "mimic" from the French word "clown" (mime). June to September.

MONKEY FLOWER,　　　*Mimulus guttatus*　　　FIGWORT FAMILY
COMMON　　　　　　　　　　　　　　　　　pl. 99

　　Monkey Flowers are distinguished by their easily recognizable shape. They are a two-lipped, five-petaled blossom of tubular shape, two lips turned up and three lips down. This yellow species can have tiny (½-inch) to quite large (2-inches) flowers. Some flowers are dotted with color and some are plain yellow. The petioles are shorter than the flower tube; multiple blossoms are located on the end of the stem. The smooth leaves are oval and opposite, on stems 4- to 36-inches tall. This **Monkey Flower** will continue to bloom as long as water is present or the ground is moist. *Mimulus* means "mimic" (as in a clown) and *guttatus* means "spotted throat." June to September.

MONKEY FLOWER,　　　*Mimulus cardinalis*　　FIGWORT FAMILY
CRIMSON　　　　　　　　　　　　　　　　　pl. 135

　　This species is characterized by its bold red color; it stands like a scarlet banner over seeps and bogs. When at its peak the blossoms are numerous and will brightly color a marshy area. The blossom is the typical **Monkey Flower** shape, except the upper lip projects forward while the lower lip is swept back, making it appear unbalanced. The yellow stamens and styles protrude beyond the petals so that it can be pollinated by the hovering Hummingbirds which are attracted to the red hue. The oval-shaped leaves are toothed and covered with sticky hairs. It grows from 4,000- to 7,000-feet. *Mimulus* means "mimic" and *cardinalis* means "red" as in the Cardinals red robe. April to September.

MONKEY FLOWER,　　　*Mimulus layneae*　　FIGWORT FAMILY
LAYNE'S　　　　　　　　　　　　　　　　　pl. 136

　　Look for this diminutive (½- to 1-inch wide) **Monkey Flower** growing out of cracks in massive granite slabs. The blossom is dark rose color with a white throat having red spots. The leaves are oval and opposite on a short 4- to 12-inch stem. Elevation ranges anywhere below 7,500-feet. May to August.

MONKEY FLOWER, PINK   *Mimulus lewisii*   FIGWORT FAMILY
pl. 133

A delicate and lovely addition to Yosemite's roadsides. Its flower shape is typical of **Monkey Flowers** but its color is a soft pink with yellow ridges running down the throat. The stems are 1- to 3-feet tall with numerous blossoms, usually in pairs. The leaves are oval, sticky haired and opposite. They can be found in moist areas, in particular, lining the rock walls along the Tioga Road just east of Yosemite Creek. *Mimulus* means "mimic" and *lewisii* is named after Captain Meriwether Lewis, of the Lewis and Clark expedition. June to August.

MONKEY FLOWER,   *Mimulus primuloides*   FIGWORT FAMILY
PRIMROSE   pl. 96

Even though the blossom has an unadorned yellow color, this **Monkey Flower** is unique in that it bears only a single blossom on each 1- to 4-inch upright stem. The leaves are in a basal rosette, very hairy, oval and toothed. It prefers moist meadows at middle elevations and blooms early, May to July, but in wet years can be seen as late as September. *Mimulus* means "mimic," *primula* "first" (to bloom).

MONKSHOOD   *Aconitum columbianum*   BUTTERCUP FAMILY
pl. 192

This flower is distinctive and uncommon enough to make it a rare and exciting treat to find. It resembles the **Larkspur** in color, leaf and plant shape, but the flower is different. Its five outer parts are sepals, not petals, the top one forming a hood over a round "head." The poisonous leaves are deeply cut into three or five segments. It can be found in wet meadows above 6,000-feet, standing 1- to 6-feet tall. *Aconitum* means **Monkshood** and *columbianum* means "Columbia River." June to August.

MOUNTAIN LADY'S   *Cypripedium montanum*   ORCHID FAMILY
SLIPPER   pl. 28

The **Lady's Slipper** is one of Nature's most unique creations! Everything about this plant is stunning. The blossom consists of three-petals, the one which is the large white "slipper" has purple veins. The two remaining petals are brown and very curly. The three brown sepals look like only two, because the lower two are united. One sepal points up while the united two droop downward. There are one to three flowers per plant, each located at the axils of the leaves. The four to seven leaves are oval shaped with coarse, linear veins, and clasp the stem. They grow to 2-feet high in moist woods at middle elevations. June to August.

MULE EARS   *Wyethia mollis*   SUNFLOWER FAMILY
pl. 87

A striking **Sunflower** cousin more recognized for its long (7- to 9-inch), hairy mule ear-like leaves than its flowers. The ray flowers are sparse (five to nine) around a center of yellow disk flowers. The flower heads usually occur just above the leaf tops. It is found from 5,000- to 10,000-feet on dry slopes and open forests. It was named after N. Wyeth, *mollis* means "soft." April to July.

MULLEIN, MOTH   *Verbascum blattaria*   FIGWORT FAMILY
pl. 64

An obscure, plain plant that seems to fade to the background among all the other brightly lit superstars of the meadows. It grows tall and slender (12- to 60-inches) rising out of a rosette of dull-toothed strap-like leaves. The flowers are pale yellow, five-lobed, reminding you of a television satellite dish looking upward. It grows along the meadow fringes and in disturbed soil. This plant is a non-native and was introduced from Eurasia. *Verbascum* means "Mullein." May to August.

MULLEIN, TURKEY   *Eremocarpus setigerus*   SPURGE FAMILY
pl. 222

This ground-hugging, silvery-green plant grows profusely along roadsides and in disturbed areas. The stems are multi-branched, lying prostrate 1- to 8-inches high, and grow 1- to 3-feet wide. The leaves are in a rosette, oval and hairy. The tiny green flowers are obscure and often go unnoticed. The Indians realized the leaves were toxic and used them to aid in their fishing, a mass of leaves in the river would stun the fish. The Greek word *eremos* means "solitary," and *karpos* means "fruit." June to October.

MULLEIN, WOOLLY   *Verbascum thapsus*   FIGWORT FAMILY
pl. 89

Throughout Yosemite Valley's meadows and lining the roadsides, are summer monuments towering above the grasses. The **Woolly Mullein** makes its presence known by sheer height alone. On top of the coarse, 2- to 7-foot stalks are dainty, yellow, five-petaled blossoms and buds. Rarely, if ever, do all the buds open at once. The leaves are broad, lancelike, and the surface feels like felt, soft and cushion-like. It was used by the early settlers for everything imaginable: "an herb for all purposes," from hair bleach, cough cure and painkiller to witchcraft preventive. *Verbascum* means "Mullein" and *thapsus* comes from an island near Sicily. There have been many attempts to eradicate this non-native exotic plant from Yosemite Valley, without success. June to September.

MUSTANG CLOVER   *Linanthus ciliatus*   PHLOX FAMILY
pl. 131

This is the showboat of all the **Gilias.** It is often called **Yellow-Throated Gilia,** for the blossoms are pink and trumpet-shaped with a contrasting yellow throat. A triangular purple design marks each petal. The leaves consist of five to eleven linear lobes that appear to be whorled around the 4- to 12-inch hairy stem. They can be found on dry, gravelly slopes at low elevations. May to July.

MUSTARD, TOWER   *Arabis glabra*   MUSTARD FAMILY
pl. 68

All of the MUSTARDS are easily recognized by their "maltese cross" shape (four-petals and four-sepals), and this one is no exception. The pale yellow blossoms are small (¾-inch) and sparsely arranged on top of tall (2- to 6-feet), spindly stems. The leaves are basal and reverse toothed. The slender seedpods stand upright and form as the flowers fade. They can be found in disturbed places and along roadsides below 7,000-feet. May to September.

ONION, SWAMP   *Allium validum*   AMARYLLIS FAMILY
pl. 163

A stroll alongside many streambanks in Yosemite can be reminiscent of shopping in the produce section of your supermarket. You'll detect a scent that is quite strong and similar to the **Green Onion.** The flower is a tight umbel of sharply pointed, elongated flowers with the stamens extending beyond the petals making it appear fuzzy. The flowers are always prominent, since it grows just slightly taller than the grasses and rushes surrounding it in its wet environment. The leaves are strap-like and thick. *Allium* means "garlic" and *validum* means "strong." There are about ten species in Yosemite, all difficult to distinguish without digging up the bulb. It added flavor to the diet of the Indians and early settlers and was prized by both. June to August.

ORCHID, GREEN REIN   *Habenaria sparsiflora*   ORCHID FAMILY
pl. 224

Another one of Yosemite's many **Orchids,** occasionally hard to find since the entire plant is a delicate green and blends nicely with the surrounding community. The stem is 12- to 24-inches tall with only a few tiny, green, Orchid-shaped blossoms scattered along its length. The leaves are lancelike and basal. It can be found in many moist mountain marshes from 6,000- to 10,000-feet. *Habenaria* is Latin for "reins" or "narrow strap" and *sparsiflora* means "spur flower." June to August.

ORCHID, PHANTOM   *Eburophyton austinae*   ORCHID FAMILY
pl. 27

ORCHIDS form the largest flower family in the world, consisting of 600 to 700 genera with over 20,000 species. Most of them are located in the tropics with only a few found in the Sierra and then only one considered common: the **Sierra Rein Orchid** *(Habenaria dilatata).* The **Phantom Orchid** has a mycorrhizal relationship with fungi (see **Pinedrops**). It has no chlorophyll and is incapable of photosynthesis, it appears a ghostly, waxy white. Each blossom has three sepals and two upper petals, all similar and lancelike. In addition, there is a yellow fleck on the lip petal. The leaves are few and are located low on the 12- to 24-inch stem. It grows in dense, moist woods, rich in humus. June to July.

ORCHID, SIERRA REIN	*Habenaria dilatata*	ORCHID FAMILY pl. 40

This elegant **Orchid,** with its beautiful, white terminal spikes, is typically found growing in the company of **Camas Lilies** and **Shooting Stars.** Each tiny white blossom has a spur petal that is much longer than the lip petal. The stem is 1- to 3-feet tall with thick lancelike leaves. It can be found wherever there are seeps, bogs or moist meadows from 4,000- to 10,000-feet. *Habenaria* means "rein," for the spurs on the flower remind you of a horse's reins, and *dilatata* means "spread out." About 11 species of Orchid are found in Yosemite Park. May to August.

OWLS CLOVER	*Orthocarpus purpurascens*	FIGWORT FAMILY pl. 141

In appearance this flower will probably remind you of its distant relative, **Lemmon's Paintbrush.** To keep you from getting confused, check your elevation. **Owls Clover** (which is not a clover at all) grows below 4,000-feet and blooms in the early spring. It can be found on grassy slopes mingling with **California Poppies** and **Lupine.** Its terminal magenta blossom is made up of many tiny flowers and leaf bracts. The blossom has a hooked beak and three lower yellow sacs. If you look closely, with some imagination, you can see the beak and eyes of an owl. It makes up for its short stature (4- to 16-inches) by filling the hillsides with color. *Orthocarpus* means "with straight fruit" and *purpurascens* "purplish." March to July.

PAINTBRUSH, ALPINE	*Castilleja nana*	FIGWORT FAMILY pl. 129

As with almost all alpine plants, this species is smaller than its lowland cousins. It has a pinkish-gray color and its leaves are directly stemmed, contoured with five to seven lobes. The tops of the flower spikes have little black tips. They prefer dry rocky alpine areas 9,000- to 12,000-feet. June to July.

PAINTBRUSH, INDIAN	*Castilleja miniata*	FIGWORT FAMILY pl. 130

This **Paintbrush's** all-red blossom is up to 2-inches long. The leaves are smooth and lancelike on erect 1- to 3-foot tall stems. It favors moist areas up to timberline. The pollinator is the Hummingbird, which is attracted to the colored blossom and has no trouble enjoying the tasty nectar. May to September.

PAINTBRUSH, LEMMON'S	*Castilleja lemmonii*	FIGWORT FAMILY pl. 132

This deep magenta flower can be found forming lush carpets of color in subalpine meadows. The leaves closest to the flower head are tri-lobed, while lower leaves are lancelike on stems that average 4-inches high. It can be found in moist meadows. **Paintbrush** quite often derives a portion of its nourishment by tapping into the root system of a nearby host. June to August.

PEA, SIERRA NEVADA	*Lathyrus nevadensis*	PEA FAMILY pl. 211

There are 22 species of **Sweet Pea** growing wild in California. Most have "escaped" from our cultivated gardens, but some are true natives. Regardless of their origins, all are lovely residents of the wild. Each has a typical "pea-shaped" flower, such as the one we described for the **Lupines.** The leaflets are oval and opposite, grouped four to eight per leaf along the creeping stems. They grow in the foothills to 5,000-feet. April to July.

PEARLY EVERLASTING   *Anaphalis margaritacea*   SUNFLOWER FAMILY
                                                                  pl. 51

The numerous oval flower heads form a 2- to 6-inch wide cluster of flowers which are predominantly white, papery bracts, interspersed with a few yellow disk flowers. The leaves are linear and alternately arranged on a single 8- to 36-inch stalk. It is fond of open woods or roadsides up to 9,000-feet. *Anaphalis* means "something everlasting" and *margaritacea* means

"pearly." The common name seems to suggest that even when dried these lovely blossoms will not wilt. Indeed, they are a distinctive addition to any dried flower arrangement. However, by mandate of the people, Yosemite is a National Park, where all living things are protected and allowed to exist naturally. Survival and reproduction demands that "no plant" be taken from its habitat. June to September.

PENNYROYAL, MOUNTAIN   *Monardella*   MINT FAMILY
                                  odoratissima   pl. 162

This is a 12- to 24-inch, bushy member of the MINT FAMILY. The flowers are 1-inch clusters of two-lipped, basket-shaped blossoms, with four protruding stamens. The "square" stem has leaves that are lancelike and opposite. It grows in small groupings along dry ridges, roadsides, trails and open forest floors. Early settlers used this plant as a tea for colds and hay fever. *Monardella* is named after the Spanish botanist, Nicolas Monardes, and it takes no imagination at all to figure out the meaning of *odoratissima,* — just take a whiff of its pungent leaves! **Pennyroyal** comes from the French words "pulial royal," because it was used as the royal remedy against fleas. June to September.

PENNYROYAL, WESTERN   *Monardella lanceolata*   MINT FAMILY
                                                                  pl. 164

The blossom of this species is similar to that of the **Mountain Pennyroyal.** The **Western Pennyroyal,** however, grows at lower elevations, and can usually be found along Highway 140 as it descends to El Portal. Its flowers sit atop erect 6- to 24-inch stems that have long, lancelike, opposite leaves. May to August.

PENSTEMON FAMILY

Penstemons are common at all elevations throughout Yosemite. They are numerous and sometimes hard to tell apart but are easily recognized as a group. The flowers form a two-lipped basket, the upper being two-lobed, the lower having three lobes. The stamens are the "basket" and give the eerie appearance of eyes staring out at the world through its colored sunlit window. *Penstemon* means "five stamens," the largest of which is sterile and bearded (hairy), hence the common name **"Beard Tongue."** The local Indians used the stringy stems to weave baskets and leaves to make a tea for a cold remedy.

PENSTEMON, BLUE   *Penstemon laetus*   FIGWORT FAMILY
                                                         pl. 200

This Penstemon grows at moderate elevations preferring open, sunny locations. The royal blue blossom is on a sticky, hairy stem 12- to 24-inches tall. The leaves are lancelike and opposite. You can find this lovely eye-catching, flower along dry roadsides and many of Yosemite's trails. *Laetus* means "gay" for the many smiles it brings to its observers. May to August.

PENSTEMON, DAVIDSON'S   *Penstemon davidsonii*   FIGWORT FAMILY
                                                                  pl. 148

This **Penstemon's** deep lavender blossoms can be so numerous that at first glance the leaves are hardly noticed. The throat and anthers are woolly haired. Even though it is short in stature

(4-to 8-inches) it appears to be a shrub growing out of a coarse woody base. Its oval and leathery leaves reduce water loss. It has adapted to high elevations and its low stature by having proportionately larger flowers to attract infrequent pollinators. June to August.

PENSTEMON, MEADOW   *Penstemon rydbergii*   FIGWORT FAMILY
                                                       pl. 199

The **Meadow Penstemon** is found around the drying edges of subalpine and alpine meadows. Its blossoms are deep blue to purple with a white throat, arranged in a whorl around the upper third of the 8- to 18-inch stem. The leaves are lancelike and opposite. A similar species is the **Sierra Penstemon** *(P. heterodoxus).* The key to distinguishing these two Penstemons is whether the flower cluster is sticky *(rydbergii)* or not *(heterodoxus)* also the elevation is lower for *P. heterodoxus.* May to August.

PENSTEMON, MOUNTAIN   *Penstemon newberryi*   FIGWORT FAMILY
PRIDE   **pl. 146**

The **Mountain Pride** rivals the **Scarlet Gilia** for lining the roadsides with intense color. It grows in clusters which resemble small shrubs, exploding in brilliant magenta. The blossoms have woolly haired anthers and a bearded throat. The leaves are coarsely toothed, tough and oval shaped. The plant grows to 18-inches tall and prefers dry, gravelly soil. June to August.

PENSTEMON, SCARLET   *Penstemon bridgesii*   FIGWORT FAMILY
                                                       pl. 145

This **Penstemon** puts on a crimson show along the Tioga Road late in the season. It grows in 12- to 36-inch shrub-like tufts from a woody base. The tubular blossoms have a lower lip that curls backward revealing five stamens. The leaves are linear and opposite along the tall stems. This plant likes dry, gravelly slopes between 5,000- and 9,000-feet. A popular location is near Yosemite Creek on Highway 120 East. Named for Thomas Bridges, a botanist, who visited Yosemite in 1857. July to August.

PHLOX, SPREADING   *Phlox diffusa*   PHLOX FAMILY
                                               pl. 17

This small shrub adds widespread beauty to otherwise bare, rocky or sandy plots at mid-to-upper elevations. The blossoms are generally five-petaled and can be pink, white or lilac. The numerous ½-inch flowers sit atop 4- to 12-inch branches with short needle-like leaves. It is an early bloomer, from June to August, depending upon the elevation. *Phlox* means "flame" (because of the bright color), and *diffusa* means "spreading."

PINEDROPS   *Pterospora andromedea*   WINTERGREEN FAMILY
                                                 pl. 160

All the non-chlorophyll-bearing members of the WINTERGREEN and ORCHID families have mycorrhizal relationships with their environment that are complex and not completely understood. **Pinedrops** are typical of these plants that are no longer considered saprophytes. The roots of the plant are intricately associated with a fungi. The fungi break down organic material in the forest soil into compounds which the plant can absorb as food. These nutrients give the plant energy to develop a flower and subsequently reproduce. In turn, the plant manufactures sugar, which the fungi need for energy to decompose the forest soil. **Pinedrops** grow in coniferous forests where heavy layers of humus cover the forest floor, a habitat for the fungi on which they depend. The woody, wand-shaped stem grows from 1- to 3-feet tall and dangles nodding bell-shaped flowers from its upper portion. As the plant matures, it exudes a sticky substance that covers both stem and flower. With the passing of summer, the plant dries intact and remains standing—a lasting monument of uniqueness. June to August.

POPPY, CALIFORNIA   *Eschscholzia californica*   POPPY FAMILY
                                                            pl. 116

This familiar flower is the official state flower of California. The four-petaled, cup-shaped blossoms respond to light, opening during the daytime and folding up on cloudy days and at night. The leaves are fern-like and lacy on stems 8- to 24-inches tall. Named after Johann

Eschscholtz, a Baltic German poet, naturalist and traveller. The Indians used the roots as a medicine for toothaches, fried the petals to make hair oil, and cooked the leaves like spinach. February to June.

POPPY, MATILIJA *Romneya coulteri* POPPY FAMILY
pl. 3

If you are driving down the Merced River canyon in late spring, look for large groupings of 4- to 6- foot, single-stemmed, white flowers leaning in the breeze. The six white petals resemble crepe paper arranged around an orange center. The leaves are gray-green and divided into three to five lobes. They are common to the brushy foothills. All California **Poppies** close at night and on cloudy days, protecting the pollen from moisture. April to May.

PRIMROSE, EVENING *Oenothera hookeri* EVENING PRIMROSE FAMILY
pl. 62

This jewel of the wildflower kingdom will put on a show before your very eyes. Its numerous buds open in the late evening, and in a matter of a few moments it produces a four-petaled, creamy yellow blossom. The flowers close up again the next morning to avoid unwanted pollinators, for it is pollinated solely by the hovering, night-flying Hawkmoth. Its trademark is a protruding symmetrical four-lobed stigma. There are many buds on the upper stem, but only a few open at any one time. In this way it spreads its wealth of color throughout the summer. The leaves are lancelike and alternate on a 3- to 5-foot stem. It covers the meadow fringes and lines roadsides. June to October.

PRIMROSE, SIERRA *Primula suffrutescens* PRIMROSE FAMILY
pl. 120

This member of the alpine community will require considerable effort to find. The striking magenta blossoms are five-petaled with a yellow throat. The stem is 2- to 4-inches tall, rising out of a tuft of spatula-shaped and fringed leaves. The plant likes the protection of rocky ledges and crevices below the slow-melting snowbanks. It was first identified by Asa Gray, in 1872 on a expedition to Clouds Rest guided by John Muir and Galen Clark. *Primula* means "first blooming" and *suffrutescens* means "woody at the base," referring to its perennial leaf tuft. July to August.

PUSSYPAWS *Calyptridium* PURSLANE FAMILY
umbellatum **pl. 174**

This delicate pink, occasionally white, cluster of flowers resembles the upturned paw of a cat. Their soft, supple texture recalls childhood memories of playing with your kitten's foot. The 2- to 10-inch prostrate stem radiates from a rosette of bright green basal leaves. Carpets of these flowers may be seen in sandy, well-drained soil along trails and roadsides, from Yosemite Valley to above timberline. *Calyptridium* means "fruit capped by petals" and *umbellatum* means "umbrella-like flower stems." The seeds of this flower are a favorite of the local chipmunks, whose seed harvesting helps disperse the plant to new locations. The flowering heads are elevated during the day and return to the ground surface at night, an act which regulates their temperature. May to August.

RAILLARDELLA, *Raillardella scaposa* SUNFLOWER FAMILY
GREENLEAF **pl. 73**

Although usually considered an alpine flower, it can be found as low as 6,000-feet. The yellow flowering head consists only of disk flowers. The 3- to 16-inch stems rise from basal, lancelike, green leaves. It likes dry, rocky ridges and gravelly areas. July to August.

RANGER BUTTONS *Sphenosciadium* CARROT FAMILY
capitellatum **pl. 48**

This is another member of the CARROT FAMILY that likes moist meadows and streambanks. It grows in a wide elevation range (4,000- to 10,000-feet) and maintains its larger size (1½- to 5-feet tall) even in the alpine, making it appear out of place with its diminutive neighbors. The flower heads are comprised of many small, individual flowers in well separated "buttonlike" umbels instead of one large, flat umbel more characteristic of the CARROT FAMILY. The overall leaf is deeply divided, with each lobe nearly linear. *Sphenosciadium* means "wedge-shaped umbel" and *capitellatum* means "small headed." VERY POISONOUS. July to August.

REDBUD, WESTERN   *Cercis occidentalis*   PEA FAMILY
                                                            pl. 180

Spring begins in the foothills with the bare branches of the **Redbud** exploding into magenta blossoms. The blossoms are boat-shaped and cover every inch of every branch with color. As the flowers fade, the round, bright spring-green leaves begin to take over. Amber seedpods eventually develop from the faded blossoms, drooping downward all summer and adding their own uniqueness to the shrub's appearance. It is found primarily along the lower Merced River, and many have been planted in Yosemite Valley. February to April.

RHUBARB, INDIAN   *Peltiphyllum peltatum*   SAXIFRAGE FAMILY
                                                             pl. 61

The Latin name refers to the shape of the leaf. *Peltiphyllum* translates as "shield leaf" and *peltatum* means "with a shield," which is precisely what the huge, cupped, serrated leaves resemble. The stalks are edible, eaten raw by local Indians when young and boiled when mature. The small, white, five-petaled blossoms are clustered on long 1- to 4-foot stems and disappear by the time the huge leaf (1- to 2-feet wide) is prominent. It can be found along streambanks from 3,000- to 6,000-feet. April to June.

ROCKFRINGE   *Epilobium obcordatum*   EVENING PRIMROSE FAMILY
                                                        pl. 185

A distant cousin to the **Fireweed, Rockfringe** is found in alpine areas huddling around boulder bases, forming a dense mat. The blossom has four double-lobed petals, and the leaves are oval and opposite on a 4- to 12-inch stem. It also has the cross-shaped stigma characteristic of the EVENING PRIMROSE FAMILY. *Epilobium* means "above ovary" and *obcordatum* means "heart shaped petals." July to September.

ROSE, WOOD   *Rosa woodsii*   ROSE FAMILY
                        var. ultramontana   **pl. 119**

Even our national flower has its counterpart in the wild. This ROSE is not as spectacular as our hybridized, cultivated species, but when found in the wilderness it can be more exciting than an entire domestic Rose garden. The pink (sometimes yellow) blossom usually has five petals, five sepals (sometimes more), is typically rose-shaped and 1- to 2-inches wide. The leaves are oval and toothed. It grows as a shrub, multi-branched and 2- to 9-feet tall. The fruit it produces are called "hips" and were used by early settlers to make a tasty jelly and an aromatic tea. It can be found growing in moist forest locations at elevations below 8,000-feet. May to July.

ROSEROOT   *Sedum rosea*   SEDUM FAMILY
                                             pl. 166

This plant is a succulent of the high mountains. It is composed of deep red rosettes of color displayed on top of stout 2- to 6-inch stems. The leaves are thick, fleshy and oval, and are distributed evenly along the stems. It's a perennial that sprouts early each spring from last year's residual rootstock. It likes moist areas at and above timberline. *Sedum* means "to soothe" and *rosea* means "rose." June to July.

ROSY EVERLASTING   *Antennaria rosea*   SUNFLOWER FAMILY
                                                          pl. 41

This relative of the **Edelweiss** never quite opens, even when at its prime. The blossoms are tiny white bracts with pink centers sitting atop 2- to 10-inch woolly stems. The leaves are spatula-shaped and grayish, alternating with additional narrow leaves on each stem. The flowers appear never to die even when the rest of the plant has long ceased living, remaining supple to the touch even in its dried stage — hence the name **"Everlasting."** They are found growing in open woodlands, meadows and alpine fields. Year around.

SELFHEAL   *Prunella vulgaris*   MINT FAMILY
                                                   pl. 208

This member of the MINT clan will remind you of wild hops. The blue, five-petaled, two-lipped flowers are grouped on a terminal spike, clustered together with brown bracts (a leaf that is often mistaken for a flower petal). The lower three lobes are spur-tipped. The leaves are oval-shaped on a 6- to 20-inch "square" stem. It can be found growing below 3,000-feet. For centuries

MINTS have been prized for their medicinal value. This one was used for sore throats and the common cold. Even the name indicates its old usage: *Prunella* (originally *brunella*) means "a sore throat" and *vulgaris* means "common." Native to Europe. May to August.

SHIELDLEAF *Streptanthus tortuosus* MUSTARD FAMILY
pl. 123

Of all the varieties of MUSTARD, this one is the most unusual. Its leaves make it most recognizable, 1- to 3-inches wide, they are round and gently back-curved clasping the stem. By mid-summer, they will turn yellow-gold and develop long arching seedpods (reminds Lynn of a scarecrow). The sometimes forgotten flowers are small, yellow or purplish, veined, urn-shaped and always have four petals and four sepals that alternate to form a cross. It grows from the foothills to timberline on rocky outcroppings and sandy dry soil. *Streptanthus* means "twisted flower" and *tortuosus* means "winding." April to July.

SHINLEAF *Pyrola picta* WINTERGREEN FAMILY
pl. 157

This is another of Yosemite's plants that has a mycorrhizal relationship with fungi (see **Pinedrops**). The flowers are cup-shaped and droop downward off the 4- to 12-inch stem. **Shinleaf** has deep-green, white-veined basal leaves. There is, however, a leafless form, *P. aphylla*, meaning "leafless," which has no chlorophyll, and derives its nourishment from fungi which break down organic material in the forest soil. It has not been determined whether a single plant can exhibit both leaf and leafless forms in its life span. Found at elevations between 4,000- and 7,000-feet. *Pyrola* means "pear-like," *picta* means "decorated" (both referring to the leaves). June to August.

SHOOTING STAR *Dodecatheon jeffreyi* PRIMROSE FAMILY
pl. 149

This wonderful flower is possibly responsible for stimulating more interest, by botany neophytes, in wildflowers than any other flower. Its unique shape, multiple colors and prolific numbers combine to transform a moist landscape into a sea of beauty. This flower can cause even the most insensitive, casual observer to appreciate the marvels of nature. The nodding blossoms have four to five petals that are curled back as if facing a constant, stiff wind. The petals are usually royal pink with bright yellow at the base with a maroon band circling the protruding stamen. It has multiple flowers at the tips of 6- to 20-inch stems, with leaves 3- to 16-inches long, spatula-shaped and basal. Found in wet areas from the foothills to the subalpine. *Dodecatheon* means "12 Gods" for it was believed 12 Greek Gods took care of this plant. May to July.

SHOOTING STAR, ALPINE *Dodecatheon alpinum* PRIMROSE FAMILY
pl. 150

A carbon-copy of the version found at lower elevations except, as its name implies, it grows in the alpine regions and is shorter (3- to 8-inches). Most alpine wildflowers compress all the color of the larger flowers into tiny blossoms that seem electric and this one is no exception. It can turn a high meadow into a neon magenta blaze between June and July.

SKY PILOT *Polemonium eximium* PHLOX FAMILY
pl. 207

The **Sky Pilot** can truly be called the "king of the mountain" sitting on the thrones of the highest and most regal peaks of the Park. In the thin air and stark rock gardens above 11,000-feet, this enticing and exquisite flower thrives where nothing else, including most people, can. The sight of this beauty, after enduring an arduous hike, is a just reward for your efforts. Springing out of the bare granite are basal, fern-like, 1- to 4-inch leaves, which are actually many three to five parted leaflets. The blossom is a cluster of five-petaled trumpets forming a bright blue head rising out of the foliage. It is a slightly sticky, pungent smelling perennial that struggles to set seed during the short alpine growing season. The name **"Skypilot"** is given to a person who leads others to heaven; *eximium* means "most beautiful." July to August.

SNEEZEWEED, BIGELOW'S   *Helenium bigelovii*   SUNFLOWER FAMILY
pl. 84

Sneezeweed resembles an upright **Sunflower,** except the flower head has dark disk flowers and the 13 to 30 ray flowers are serrated and droop downward. The singular flowers sit atop 24- to 36-inch stems with 4- to 10-inch lancelike leaves. Large groupings of these pretty yellow flowers seem to blow in unison with gentle breezes of the summer afternoons. They grow in moist meadow areas from 3,000- to 8,000-feet. Contrary to its name, it rarely inflicts an allergic reaction. The name seems to come from the early settlers' use of powdered, dried flowers to induce sneezing to help clear head colds. *Helenium* is named after "Helen of Troy" and *bigelovii* after the eighteenth century botanist, Dr. John Bigelow. June to August.

SNOW PLANT   *Sarcodes sanguinea*   WINTERGREEN FAMILY
pl. 159

This plant has no chlorophyll and is incapable of photosynthesis. It can be found growing in the decaying humus of coniferous forests, and has a mycorrhizal relationship with fungi (see **Pinedrops**). Contrary to its name's suggestion, it does not associate with snow, unless taken by a surprise spring snow fall. It initially is pyramidal in shape, with long fingerlike twisting scales wrapping the plant in its single color of flaming red to salmon pink. As the plant matures, the scales loosen and part, revealing nodding, delicate, urn-shaped blossoms ½- to ¾-inch long. Great care need be taken with this scarce and unusual plant, so we remind you to look, don't touch and leave them for someone else to enjoy now and in the future. The Latin name means "blood-red." May to July.

SNOWBERRY, PARISH'S   *Symphoricarpos parishii*   HONEYSUCKLE FAMILY
pl. 58

This shrub-like creeper has leaves more prominent than its tiny blossoms. In August the fruit appears as large white berries. The flowers are tubular, creamy-white to pink, located at the intersection of the upper leaves and stems. The gray-green leaves are oval and opposite on the 24-to 36-inch long stems. It likes dry slopes from 4,000- to 10,000-feet and can be found along Highway 41 just north of Chinquapin. June to August.

SORREL, MOUNTAIN   *Oxyria digyna*   BUCKWHEAT FAMILY
pl. 217

The only way to see this beauty is to lace up your boots and hike above timberline. It is a hardy little (2- to 10-inch) addition to the stark, open rock fields of the alpine zone. From out of the kidney-shaped basal leaves rises the stem with a cluster of red or green ¼-inch flowers hanging from the upper half. It likes to grow in crevices and behind rocks where it is sheltered from the constant summer winds. *Oxyria* means "sour" and *digyna* means "with two pistils." July to September.

SPEARMINT   *Mentha spicata*   MINT FAMILY
pl. 176

The MINT FAMILY is a widespread herb that, historically, has been prized both as a flavoring and a medicine. **Spearmint** has traditionally been the most sought after of the MINT FAMILY. The flowers are a terminal cluster of tiny, five-petaled, two-lipped flowers. The flowering spike is located well above the wrinkled, lancelike leaves and the "square" stem stands 1- to 4-feet high. It grows in thickets, forming a natural aromatic hedge. The **Spearmint** is a native of Europe. Look for it in moist places at all elevations below 8,000-feet. June to October.

SPICE BUSH   *Calycanthus*   CALYCANTHUS FAMILY
occidentalis   pl. 178

Although this is a shrub, it evokes as much interest as any wildflower, standing up to 12-feet tall with intense green, oval leaves and spaced daintily along the branches, are bright red flowers. When they wilt in late summer and brown, thimble-shaped seedpods take their place. *Calycanthus* like the lower Merced River area along the moist banks. The name was given for the spicy fragrance of the leaves and the wine-like fragrance of the flower. This odor attracts its main pollinator, the beetle. The CALYCANTHUS is a very primitive family. It is believed that the first flowering plants that appeared on earth resembled families like CALYCANTHUS and MAGNOLIA. If you look closely at the flower you can see how its parts may have been derived from the leaves. May to July.

SPIRAEA   *Spiraea densiflora*   ROSE FAMILY
                                                       pl. 165

Spiraea is a shrub that loves the moist rocky areas below melting snow or seeps. It will grow to a height of 36-inches with closely grouped stems. The blossoms adorning the tips consist of many tiny flowers grouped together, while the protruding stamens give the overall blossom a fuzzy appearance. It grows best in middle to upper elevations and is usually seen in rock crevices. July to August.

ST. JOHN'S WORT   *Hypericum formosum*   ST. JOHN'S WORT FAMILY
                          var. scouleri   **pl. 71**

This plant is a European import that seems to be an average, ho-hum flower, until one looks closer. This vibrant yellow, five-petaled flower can liven up an otherwise mundane meadow. Accenting the flower are many stamens, which give it a prickly appearance. Several blossoms are attached to the upper end of 10- to 20-inch stems. The leaves are 1-inch long, lancelike, and dotted black. It prefers moist meadows at middle elevations, especially in Yosemite Valley. The name, **St. John's Wort,** comes from Europe, where it seemed to blossom on June 24, the day dedicated to St. John the Baptist. June to September.

STEERS HEAD   *Dicentra uniflora*   BLEEDINGHEART FAMILY
                                                       pl. 139

The joy of seeing your first **Steers Head** will never be forgotten, for it truly is a precious treasure to find. Appearing between 7,000- and 10,000-feet after the snows melt, this tiny, tiny plant emerges to a total height of 1- to 4-inches. It has only one flower, separate from its leaf, but sharing the same rootstock. The leaves are tiny, elaborate, lacy and pinnate. The stunning pink or white flower is four-petaled, two-sepaled, which jointly forms the shape of a sunbleached steer's skull. It is not a rare flower, but because of its short growing time, you have to be at the right place at the right time (just after the snow melts). Two of the places to see this flower are the top of Illilouette Falls and the western slopes of Mt. Dana. *Dicentra* means "two-spurred" and *uniflora* means "single-flowered." March to June.

STEPHANOMERIA   *Stephanomeria*   SUNFLOWER FAMILY
                          tenuifolia   **pl. 170**

This plant would often be overlooked except for the pink-to-purple ray flowers. The stems are tall and branched near the base with few, small, linear leaves. Since the spindly stems fade against the dry, rocky habitat, the sparse flowers appear to "float" in mid air. You can find them on Highway 120 near the tunnels (Lynn nicknamed them **"Tunnel Flowers"**). July to August.

STICKSEED, VELVETY   *Hackelia velutina*   BORAGE FAMILY
                                                       pl. 177

Its flowers are bright blue, ¾-inch wide, five-petaled with five scales at the throat. The blossoms usually cluster at the top of 12- to 24-inch stems with lancelike leaves. The fruit has flat, barbed hooks surrounding it which allow it to be easily picked up by a passerby, hence the name **"Stickseed."** It can be found in open woods and along roadsides from 4,000- to 8,000-feet. *Hackelia* is named after the German agriculturalist, Joseph Hackel, and *velutina* means "velvety." June to August.

STONECROP   *Sedum obtusatum*   SEDUM FAMILY
                                                       pl. 109

You will find this delicate little succulent growing from cracks and crevices. The thick, fleshy leaves form a mat of basal rosettes from which a bright red 2- to 6-inch stem rises. The early blossoms are yellow but will fade to pink as the season progresses. It can be found from 4,000-feet to timberline. May to August.

STRAWBERRY, WILD   *Fragaria californica*   ROSE FAMILY
                                                       pl. 10

You may discover sweet and delicious berries on this low-growing creeper if they have survived the harvesting by the animals and birds that delight in its tiny fruit. Like a typical cultivated **Strawberry,** the rootstocks are perennial and produce runners (elongated stems) that root at their tips and produce new **Strawberry** plants. In this way, a single plant can expand over a considerable area without sexual reproduction. The flowers are a delicate five-petaled blossom and the leaves are three-lobed and sharply toothed. March to July.

SULPHUR FLOWER   *Eriogonum umbellatum*   BUCKWHEAT FAMILY
                                                            pl. 105

This is one of the most common and most colorful plants found bordering dry, sandy roads and trails. A myriad of gray stems, 4- to 12-inches tall, rise out of clustered rosettes of small leaves. Each 1-inch blossom has an umbrella-like head made up of many tiny flowers varying in color from bright yellow (most common) to burnt orange. 6,000- to 9,000-feet. July to August.

SUNFLOWER, COMMON   *Helianthus annuus*   SUNFLOWER FAMILY
                                                            pl. 81

The **Common Sunflower** is the textbook example of the second largest family in the botanical kingdom, with over 920 genera and 19,000 species worldwide. This simple, recognizable flower (3- to 5-inches wide) has many yellow ray flowers and maroon disk flowers. The 2- to 6-foot stem usually branches and a single plant can have many flowers. The leaves are oval with irregular teeth and are hairy, as is the stem. An impressive grouping is located along the road near the Ahwahnee Hotel just before the entrance gate. It was introduced from the northern midwest and has become another Yosemite Valley weed. The Greek word *helios* means "sun" and *anthos*, "flower" (because the flower-heads face the sun). July to September.

SUNFLOWER, WOOLLY   *Eriophyllum lanatum*   SUNFLOWER FAMILY
                                                              pl. 83

This bright yellow, multi-headed flower brightens many areas along the Tioga Road. It is a Sunflower-type blossom that has both ray flowers (8 to 13) and disk flowers. The name reflects the fuzziness of the leaves and stem. It favors any rocky area below 9,000-feet. *Eriophyllum* means "woolly leaf" and *lanatum* "woolly stem." June to August.

THIMBLEBERRY   *Rubus parviflorus*   ROSE FAMILY
                                                       pl. 2

This plant is a delightful encounter, especially when the fruit is mature. If you can beat the bears and the birds, you'll find the bright red berries are quite tasty. The five-petaled, white, papery blossoms are scattered throughout the 2- to 7-foot shrubby plant. The leaves are very large (up to 12-inches across) with three to five pointed lobes. It frequents moist streambanks at most elevations. Blooms July to August. Fruits in August.

THISTLE, BULL   *Cirsium vulgare*   SUNFLOWER FAMILY
                                                      pl. 204

The **Thistle** is often looked upon as a dreaded pest and a misencounter can certainly be quite painful. Stoneman Meadow is an especially good place to see this **Thistle** in great numbers, for it is replacing native plants in Yosemite Valley and is considered a terrible weed. The hour-glass-shaped flower sits atop a 2- to 4-foot coarse stem. The head appears to be a rounded, tight grouping of purple spines (like an old fashioned shaving brush) on top of a green, thorny receptacle. The leaves are long and deeply cut, making them appear maple-leaved with many sharp spines. Grows up to 9,000-feet. *Cirsium* means "swollen veins" (extracts were made for treating swollen veins), *vulgare* means "common." June to September.

THISTLE, DRUMMOND'S   *Cirsium drummondii*   SUNFLOWER FAMILY
                                                               pl. 21

This spiny ground-hugging thistle with white flower heads nestled in a rosette of leaves is found in meadows and on disturbed ground below 8,000-feet. Its cousin, *C. tioganum,* is more striking (though very similar) and grows at higher elevations. The name *Cirsium* is a Greek word meaning "swollen veins," as the plant was used as a remedy for this ailment. June to August.

THISTLE, PEREGRINE   *Cirsium cymosum*   SUNFLOWER FAMILY
                                                           pl. 18

Less common than the **Bull Thistle** *(C. vulgare)*, this **Thistle** is white to creamy-white and can be found in the meadows of Yosemite Valley. The receptacle has shiny green phyllaries. The leaves are sparse, lancelike and spiny on gray 2- to 5-foot tall stems. The phyllaries are similar to the leaves you eat on its cousin the **Artichoke.** When the **Thistle** is not in bloom, the immature beginnings of the ray and disk flowers are called "pappus" are equivalent to the hairs above the heart of an **Artichoke** (that you scoop out and throw away). The Greek word *Kirsion* was a name for a kind of **Thistle.** June to September.

THISTLE, YELLOW STAR   *Centaurea solstitialis*   SUNFLOWER FAMILY
                                                          pl. 76

This little **Thistle** has two prominent features: a vibrant yellow flower head pointing upward and long, perpendicular, vicious spines arranged in a wheel around its base. The blossoms are placed atop a 1- to 5-foot stem with linear leaves. It is found along the road from El Portal to Yosemite Valley. It is one of the most noxious weeds of the area and is replacing many of the native plants in Yosemite Valley. June to September.

TINCTURE PLANT   *Collinsia tinctoria*   FIGWORT FAMILY
                                                 pl. 34

This is a later blooming, creamy version of its purple cousin, **Chinese Pagodas** *(C. heterophylla).* It grows in such masses that it appears to be a creeper. However, each is a singular 2- to 8-inch plant clustered to form a white and blue carpet. The blossoms are two-lipped and whorled symmetrically around the stem, growing smaller toward the tip and appearing pagoda-like. The upper lip is white with a yellow base which has blue speckles and the lower lip is purple-veined. The leaves are oval and opposite. It grows on meadow fringes and on sandy flats, 2,000- to 6,000-feet. *Collinsia* is named after an eighteenth century American botanist, Zaccheus Collins; *tinctoria* means "dyeing" for when the plant is broken it emits a brown stain. One impressive display is located in the northwest corner of El Capitan Meadow. June to August.

TINKERS PENNY   *Hypericum anagalloides*   ST. JOHN'S WORT FAMILY
                                                   pl. 70

If you are accustomed to seeing others in this family, you will undoubtedly overlook **Tinkers Penny.** It is a tiny creeper whose overall plant size is usually only 2- to 6-inches in diameter. The ¼-inch blossoms are diminutive replicas of its larger cousin, **St. John's Wort.** The paired leaves are oval-shaped on a 3-inch stem, with the orange-yellow flowers near the end. It can be found bordering moist meadows at all elevations. June to August.

TRILLIUM, GIANT   *Trillium chloropetalum*   LILY FAMILY
                                                     pl. 156

This is an early-blooming forest dweller with leaves that can be more impressive than the blossom. The flowers number three (Trillium) and are broadly oval (almost triangular) with purple mottling. The red-to-maroon lancelike petals point upward at the axil of the leaves. The plant does have an 8- to 24-inch stem, but leaves appear to rise directly from the soil. It can be found in dense, moist forests. February to May.

VERBENA, WESTERN   *Verbena lasiostachys*   VERVAIN FAMILY
                                                    pl. 213

This plant appears to be a **Mint,** but note the distinctly different aroma. The leaves are long, narrow and tri-lobed on a "square," 1- to 3-foot stem. The blue flowers are sparse on a long, terminal spike. The blossoms are tubular, five-petaled and two-lipped, the upper top having two petals and the lower three petals. They can be found along roadsides and disturbed places. July to September.

VIOLET, MACLOSKEY'S   *Viola macloskeyi*   VIOLET FAMILY
                                                   pl. 29

The flower of this common, white **Violet** is five-petaled. The top two petals are turned downward and the bottom three petals are purple-veined. Leaves are triangular- to kidney-shaped. It grows from 1- to 5-inches tall in wet meadows. June to August.

VIOLET, MOUNTAIN   *Viola purpurea*   VIOLET FAMILY
                                              pl. 100

Highly prized for their uncommon beauty, VIOLETS are found worldwide. Yosemite, too, has its prized VIOLETS, the most common being the bright yellow **Mountain Violet.** The flower has five petals, two on the upper side and three on the lower; this species has purple stripes on the lower lobes. Its stem rises 2- to 6-inches from a rosette of deep-green triangular leaves. You can find it on humus rich slopes and flats early in the season. April to June.

131

VIOLET, WESTERN   *Viola adunca*   VIOLET FAMILY
pl. 209

Another wild variety of a genus the world has cultivated for centuries. The blossom is five-petaled with the spur being almost as long as the rest of the flower. It is usually deep or pale blue but occasionally white. The leaves are oval on stems only 2- to 6-inches high. It frequents wet open woods. *Viola* means "violet" and *adunca* means "hooked." April to September.

WALLFLOWER, SIERRA   *Erysimum perenne*   MUSTARD FAMILY
pl. 91

This striking cluster of four-petaled, four-sepaled bright yellow flowers, forming a cross typical of the MUSTARD FAMILY and sits atop a 4- to 12-inch stem. Its spatula-shaped leaves are arranged singularly. It is usually found in high-elevation forests up to and above timberline. The long seedpods, forming before the blossoms wane, are another of the characteristics of the MUSTARD FAMILY. June to August.

WALLFLOWER, WESTERN   *Erysimum capitatum*   MUSTARD FAMILY
pl. 92

This plant adds a dash of color (yellow, orange, red or maroon depending on the elevation) to stony outcroppings below 8,000-feet. The flowers are a cluster of four-petaled blossoms arranged in a sphere-shape on top of a stout 12- to 24-inch stem. The leaves are lancelike and slightly toothed. April to July.

WOODLAND STAR   *Lithophragma affinis*   SAXIFRAGE FAMILY
pl. 38

The white to pink toothy blossoms are found sparsely arranged on the hairy, 6- to 24-inch stem. The leaves are basal and rounded, just slightly divided. It is found in grassy places and open woods in middle to lower elevations. Greek *Lithos* means "rock;" *phragma,* "fence" (referring to its habitat). April to June.

WILLOW, ALPINE   *Salix anglorum*   WILLOW FAMILY
ssp. *antiplasti*   pl. 57

This is a true **Willow,** tiny enough to be obscure to all but the most dedicated searcher. The leaves are typically oval on small branches that lie prostrate, forming a ground cover. The catkins are upright, as high as 3-inches and appear woolly. Its seeds are dispersed in the constant alpine winds. It can be found readily around Vogelsang High Sierra Camp and other alpine meadows, 9,500- to 12,000-feet. *Salix:* Latin for "willow." July to August.

YAMPAH   *Perideridia bolanderi*   CARROT FAMILY
pl. 45

When you encounter an "ocean" of white lace in a mountain meadow, it will most often be **Yampah.** It is hard to overlook when found in such exquisite abundance, for the flowers are actually the lacework of many tiny flowers, clustered in an umbel up to 3-inches across. The stems are 8- to 30-inches tall and almost leafless. Those leaves that are apparent are slender and divided. Indians used the tubers for food and it was the Shoshone Indians that named this plant. *Perideridia* means "necklace" and *bolanderi* is named after Henry Bolander, the California state botanist in 1864. May to August.

YARROW   *Achillea lanulosa*   SUNFLOWER FAMILY
pl. 42

Yarrow is seldom overlooked by visitors since it is quite common and has a long-lasting blossom. It is a flat-topped, terminal cluster of tiny flower heads less than ¼-inch across, making it appear to be a single 2-inch blossom. The leaves are also quite distinctive, in both shape and pungent odor. The leaves are linear and highly dissected to give them a fern-like appearance. **Yarrow** grows in open flats to timberline. *Achillea comes from Achilles,* the Greek hero. He is said to have healed his wounded soldiers with an ointment made from the leaves. The Indians, also, used it to cure toothaches, headaches and stomachaches; *lanulosa* means "woolly." April to September.

132

GLOSSARIES

WRITTEN
AND
ILLUSTRATED

GLOSSARY

ACHENE OR AKENE	the small, dry and hard one-seeded fruit
ALP	a high mountain meadowland
ANNUAL	a plant that lasts only one season
ANTHER	the part of the stamen that bears the pollen
AXIL	the angle formed by the base of a leaf, with the stem
BANNER	the upper petal of a flower in the pea family
BASAL	located at the base
BERRY	a fleshy fruit with multiple seeds
BRACT	a modified leaf growing under a flower or cluster of flowers, as in the Pacific Dogwood
CALYX	*Oh!* ← → plural of sepal
CATKIN	a dense, elongated cluster of unisexual flowers; as in the Willow or Oak
CLASPING	partially surrounding the stem
COMPOUND	with leaves, having two or more similar lobes
COROLLA	plural of petals, especially those that are partially joined
DISK FLOWER	the tubular flowers located in the center of a composite (sunflower family)
EVERGREEN	retaining its leaves all year
FILAMENT	the thin stalk portion of the stamen
FLOWER	the reproductive organ of a large group of plants
FRUIT	a mature seed or berry; the product of the reproduction cycle of a plant
HABITAT	the environment in which a plant grows
KEEL	the fused bottom two petals of a flower in the pea family
LEAFLET	one of the appendages of a compound leaf
NODDING	hanging downward
OVARY	the part of the pistil that contains the seed or seeds

134

PALMATE	a leaf that has the lobes radiating from a common point
PAPPUS	the whole of bristles at the apex of the single, hard seed of the sunflower family
PEDICEL	the stem of a single flower
PERENNIAL	a plant that continues to live from one season to the next
PETAL	the part of a flower, usually colored, that attracts your attention; the portion that makes up the corolla
PETIOLE	the stem of a leaf
PINNATE	a leaf that has its leaflets arranged on either side of the central axis
PISTIL	the female, seed bearing organ of a flower
PROSTRATE	growing flat on the ground
RAY FLOWER	the flat, elongated flowers arranged on the margin of a composite (sunflower family)
RECEPTACLE	in the composite (sunflower) family, the fleshy base
RECURVED	bent back on itself
ROOTSTOCK	the underground root-like stem
ROSETTE	an arrangement of leaves in a circular pattern around the base of a plant
SEPAL	the parts of a flower below the petals, usually green
STAMEN	the male part of the flower which bears the pollen
STYLE	the thin, tubular portion of a pistil between the ovary and the stigma
TERMINAL SPIKE	a tight arrangement of flowers located at the end of the stem
TOOTHED	leaves that have coarse serrations along the margin
UMBEL	(umbrella-shaped) a flat or semi-circular cluster of flowers forming an upside down umbrella radiating from a common stem
WING	the outer petals of a flower in the pea family

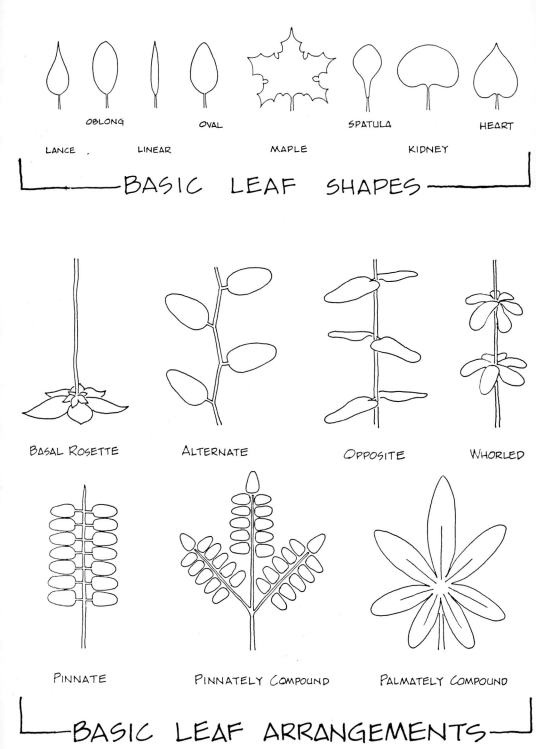

OBLONG OVAL SPATULA HEART

LANCE LINEAR MAPLE KIDNEY

BASIC LEAF SHAPES

BASAL ROSETTE ALTERNATE OPPOSITE WHORLED

PINNATE PINNATELY COMPOUND PALMATELY COMPOUND

BASIC LEAF ARRANGEMENTS

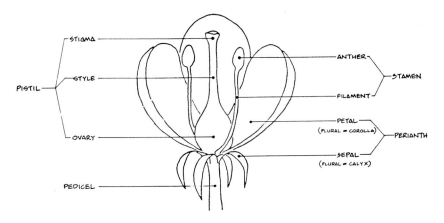

STIGMA

STYLE

PISTIL

OVARY

PEDICEL

ANTHER
STAMEN
FILAMENT

PETAL
(PLURAL = COROLLA)
PERIANTH
SEPAL
(PLURAL = CALYX)

BASIC FLOWER PARTS

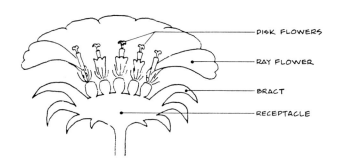

DISK FLOWERS

RAY FLOWER

BRACT

RECEPTACLE

COMPOSITE FLOWER PARTS

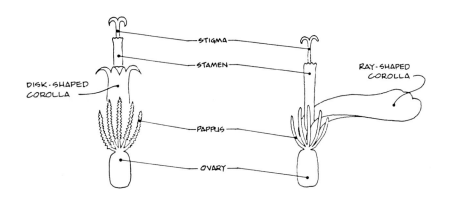

STIGMA

STAMEN

DISK-SHAPED
COROLLA

RAY-SHAPED
COROLLA

PAPPUS

OVARY

DISK FLOWER   RAY FLOWER

BIBLIOGRAPHY

Abrams, LeRoy — Illustrated Flora of the Pacific States
Stanford University Press, 1940, 1950, 1951, and 1960 (4 vols.)

Botti, Stephen J. and Mendershausen, Ann
Wildflowers of the Hite's Cove Trail
Pioneer Publishing Co., 1985

Browning, Peter — Place Names of the Sierra Nevada
Wilderness Press, 1986

Hall, Harvey Monroe — Wildflowers of the Sierra Nevada
Yosemite Natural History Association, 1912

Hood, Bill and Mary — Yosemite Wildflowers and Their Stories
Flying Spur Press, 1969

Hubbard, Douglass — Wildflowers of the Sierra Nevada
Yosemite Natural History Association

Jepson, Willis Linn — Manual of the Flowering Plants of California
University of California Press, 1925 and 1953

Lloyd, Francis E. — Flowers of the Foothills
Tulip Press, 1973

Morgenson, Dana C. — Yosemite Wildflower Trails
Yosemite Natural History Association, 1975

Munz, Phillip A. — A California Flora and Supplement
University of California Press, 1973

Niehaus, Theodore F. — A Field Guide to Pacific States Wildflowers
Houghton Mifflin Co., 1976

Niehaus, Theodore F. — Sierra Wildflowers
University of California Press, 1974

Pusateri, Samuel J. Ph.D. — Flora of Our Sierran National Parks
Carl and Irving Printers, 1963

Spellenberg, Richard — Field Guide to North American Wildflowers
The Audubon Society, Chanticleer Press, 1979

Venning, Frank D. — Wildflowers of North America
Western Publishing Inc., 1984

Weeden, Norman F. — A Sierra Nevada Flora
Wilderness Press, 1975 and 1981

COMMON NAME INDEX
Bold numbers indicate color plate number.
Light face is page number.

140

SCIENTIFIC NAME INDEX
Bold numbers indicate color plate number.
Light face is page number.

Philadelphus lewisii	**53**	119
Phlox diffusa	**17**	124
Pholistoma auritum	**214**	108
Phyllodoce breweri	**153**	111
Polemonium eximium	**207**	127
Polygonum bistortoides	**44**	100
Potentilla fruticosa	**111**	103
Potentilla glanulosa	**8**	104
Potentilla gracilis	**63**	103
Primula suffrutescens	**120**	125
Prunella vulgaris	**208**	126
Pterospora andromedea	**160**	124
Pyrola picta	**157**	127
Raillardella scaposa	**13**	125
Ranunculus hystriculus	**5**	102
Rhododendron occidentale	**55**	99
Romneya coulteri	**3**	125
Rosa woodsii		
var. ultramontana	**119**	126
Rubus parviflorus	**2**	130
Rudbeckia californica	**88**	105
Rudbeckia hirta	**85**	100
Salix anglorum ssp. antiplasti	**57**	132
Sambucus caerulea	**60**	108
Sarcodes sanguinea	**59**	128
Sedum obtusatum	**109**	129
Sedum rosea	**166**	126
Senecio integerrimus	**104**	111
Senecio triangularis	**108**	111
Sidalcea glaucescens	**121**	103
Silene californica	**126**	112
Sisyrinchium bellum	**183**	101
Smilacina racemosa	**31**	108
Solidago canadensis	**94**	111
Solidago multiradiata	**93**	111
Solidago occidentalis	**90**	111
Sphenosciadium capitellatum	**48**	125
Spiraea densiflora	**165**	129
Spiranthes romanzoffiana	**39**	113
Stachys albens	**32**	112
Stephanomeria tenuifolia	**170**	129
Streptanthus tortuosus	**123**	126
Symphoricarpos parishii	**58**	128
Taraxacum officinale	**78**	106
Thalictrum fendleri	**218**	118
Trichostema lanceolatum	**191**	101
Trifolium pratense	**144**	104
Trifolium repens	**22**	104
Trifolium tridentatum	**143**	104
Trillium chloropetalum	**156**	131
Vaccinium nivictum	**155**	100
Veratrum californicum	**37**	114
Verbascum blattaria	**64**	120
Verbascum thapsus	**89**	121
Verbena lasiostachys	**213**	131
Viola adunca	**209**	132
Viola macloskeyi	**29**	131
Viola purpurea	**100**	131
Wyethia mollis	**87**	120
Zauschneria californica	**142**	109
Zigadenus venenosus	**43**	106